CW00568245

Clara Schumann

Clara Schumann

Monica Steegmann

HAUS PUBLISHING · LONDON

First published in Great Britain in 2004 by
Haus Publishing Limited
26 Cadogan Court, Draycott Avenue
London SW3 3BX

A CIP catalogue record for this book is available from the British Library

ISBN 1-904341-59-4

Designed and typeset in Garamond by
Palimpsest Book Production Limited, Polmont, Stirlingshire

Printed and bound by Graphicom in Vicenza, Italy

Contents

Preparing for Life as a Musician

The physical likeness has been captured in the relief, but the spirit is lacking. *The rest is poetic, tender and delicately executed.* 'The relief' is Robert Schumann's profile, 'the rest' are the angel muses, and Clara, a muse herself, sitting at his feet. She is depicted life-size, robed like the Madonna, gazing up at him from a suitable distance, and holding a sheet of music in one hand, and his laurel wreath in the other. Clara Schumann attended the dedication of the Robert Schumann Memorial in the Bonn cemetery on a calm and sunny morning, 2 May 1880, with feelings both of *joy and sorrow* (L3,408). She had no idea that biographers of both Robert and herself, with just one exception, would take their cues from this monument right up to the end of the next century – Clara as the muse inspiring a dream partnership in music, the loving wife of Robert the Romantic hero, the woman whose life really begins with her marriage and usually ends after his death, in a sort of biographical suttee. There was of course also the opposite point of view, the provincial verdict, in which the true and caring wife becomes the spouse completely devoid of understanding, where the exemplary mother becomes the career-minded egoist. In both cases, Clara's merits as an artist in her own right are overlooked.

It was only in the 1990s that critical attention returned to the biography of Clara Schumann with which it all began – the 1908 work in three volumes by Berthold Litzmann, with the subtitle 'The Life of an Artist'. Several major studies followed – on the composer Clara Wieck-Schumann by Janina Klassen, and on Clara as pianist by Claudia de Vries; in other words, on that most important aspect of Clara, her life as an artist.

When she was just eighteen she realised *that I would be unhappy if I were unable to practise my art for ever* (S24). She found after Robert's death *how necessary music is in my life – if I had to give it up now I should soon perish* (H161). Even when she was seventy, the thought that she might no longer be able to play was completely unbearable: *How should I go on living if I had to give it up entirely!* (L3,517). Nothing shook her hold on life as strongly as the thought of giving up her music. It was something innate rather than acquired, a form of artistic expression, the language most familiar to her, *the air in which I breathe* (B1,599). *Only music and people could warm my heart* – and in that order (K75).

She was well aware who had enabled her to reach this achievement: that *genius of a teacher*, that *understanding father*, whom she *was so fortunate to have, who cared for her health* so that she *never practised too much at any one time . . . in short, who watched over her.* Even though many *call him a tyrant – it is to him that I owe that freshness that has stayed with me into my old age (at least in terms of my art)!* (L3,122,302,585) Even when they had their bitterest disputes she would remember that Friedrich Wieck had not only given her something that would be *her comfort in all times of suffering* (S196) – he also gave her what she needed for her professional success.

Nothing in Friedrich Wieck's background suggested a career as a notable teacher, piano maker and music dealer. He was born in 1785 in Pertzsch on the Elbe, some 45 kilometres from Leipzig, the son of an unsuccessful merchant. His musical aptitude was apparent early on, but the poor circumstances in which his family lived, coupled with his own weak constitution, meant he did not receive regular tuition. He was a pupil at the Thomas School in Leipzig for just six weeks, and had only a handful of piano lessons from the well-known teacher, Johann Peter Milchmeyer, who happened to be visiting Torgau where Wieck attended the Gymnasium school. These were sufficient to kindle a passionate interest in music and in piano technique. He completed his studies in Protestant theology, as his mother wished, his father having died, but he never became a pastor. Instead he became tutor to the family of Baron von Seckendorff in Querfurth, where he made friends with the music teacher Adolph Bargiel, who would later marry Wieck's first wife.

Friedrich Wieck was conscientious, intelligent and had an enquiring mind. He made a detailed study of the teaching methods of the Enlightenment by Johann Bernhard Basedow and Johann Heinrich Pestalozzi, as well as studying Jean-Jacques Rousseau. He was later to apply these in his piano lessons: the playful and individual nature of learning, enthusiasm for work and pleasure in physical training. It must have been his tireless love of learning, his passion for music, that enabled him, although self-taught, to become a reasonable pianist and a teacher of note. It is not clear, even now, how he acquired his knowledge of composition, but however it was, he sent some of his own songs to Carl Maria von Weber, who took them seriously and made lengthy comments on them. They were even discussed in the *Allgemeine Musikalische Zeitung*. Encouraged by his public recognition as a musician, and with financial help from friends, Wieck decided to resign from his job as a tutor and set up on his own.

It was a good time to start a business in Leipzig. The Battle of Leipzig in Saxony (1813) was two years in the past, and Leipzig, with its 40,000 inhabitants, was now growing into an important business and cultural centre once again. In 1815 Wieck opened a music business on the Neumarkt, where he also gave lessons, and soon earned a reputation as a capable businessman. His choice of the highly gifted Marianne Tromlitz as his wife was advantageous to him in musical circles: her grandfather, Johann Georg Tromlitz, was a well-known musician and flute-maker, while her father was Kantor of Plauen.

Marianne Tromlitz was only nineteen when they married in 1816, but she was already showing her potential as a pianist and singer. In the years that followed she appeared many times at the Gewandhaus, where her lively performance and her personality brought her success. They were only married for eight years, but in that time she gave birth to five children, ran the household, gave singing and piano lessons, helped in the business, entertained guests and prepared for her concerts. Her ability to withstand these pressures and attain success in all areas of her life were those that would later be required of her daughter Clara in her own married life.

We can only guess at the reasons why this marriage broke down. It would seem that Wieck had a violent temper and disliked interference and arguments. Marianne Tromlitz herself was tough, independent and proud. Years later Wieck had to admit: 'She was not humiliated in the slightest, although she expects trouble from that weak and sickly Bargiel' (T6,100). Wieck expected other qualities from 'womenfolk', so for him altercations and tension were soon just part of everyday life. This can be seen in his relationship with Clara too: when he was accused of letting his eight-year-old daughter play too much, he reacted 'heatedly', as he would only take 'advice on bringing up children . . . especially from women' when he asked for it (T2,97). He found Clara to be 'pig-headed' (T1,34) and 'contradictory without reason', mostly when she was disobedient and 'no longer shows the slightest interest in music', for whatever reason that might be (F51). The marriage with Wieck must have been so intolerable that Marianne Tromlitz even agreed to abandon her children when she separated from him. They were divorced in January 1825. She married their friend, the music teacher Adolph Bargiel, several months later.

Wieck's and Tromlitz's daughter Clara, 'the bright, or radiant child', was born on 13 September 1819. She was their second child (the first having died), and was born in the same year as the poet Theodor Fontane. From birth she was destined by her father for a great artistic career, to be directed by him, but in her first years she had to watch the breakdown of her parents' marriage and the disrespectful way Wieck treated her mother. The lack of harmony at home, and the silence of her nursery-maid, Johanna Strobel (to whom Clara dedicated a waltz when she was ten, although Johanna had left the family in 1825, dismissed by Wieck), may have caused Clara's muteness and her apparent deafness. She had still not spoken a single word at the age of four, a condition that was only resolved when she was eight. She was surrounded by singing and piano-playing, and the language of music, and she had no trouble in adopting these sounds, rather than words. At four years old she could reproduce tunes and short pieces at the piano by ear without difficulty. Her innate familiarity with music as a natural means of expression must have been developed even then. Later it grew into an almost insatiable need for music.

When Marianne Wieck separated from her husband she was permitted to take Clara, then aged four and a half, with her, until her fifth birthday. It was only after Wieck had demanded her return that lessons with her father began in earnest. *On 18 September (1824) my father actually began to teach me the piano. I had easily learned some exercises without moving my hand several months before I went with my mother to Plauen, and I had played by ear some easy accompaniments for dancing* (T1,5). This was noted by Wieck in her diary, writing in Clara's name as he did until May 1831. The diary was kept by them both until July 1838. It would seem that her mother had let her practise with a chiroplast, following the methods of Johann Bernard Logier. This was an apparatus attached to the piano to train finger dexterity while holding the hand still.

Wieck only used the Logier system intermittently. His teaching method was an holistic approach, that adapted to the

Her mother, Marianne Wieck, née Tromlitz. Reproduction of a portrait in a private collection.

Her father, Friedrick Wieck. Painting by an unknown artist.

individuality of his pupils, and even placed finger exercises in a musical context. He taught music as a sensual experience through touch and emotion. He applied this to ear training, to note reading, to rhythm, tone and the nature of chords and harmonies. He watched the capacity for work and independence of thought in his pupils, and helped them to develop their feelings and their sense of beauty. Major and minor scales and triads in every position, as learned by Clara, were not only for finger dexterity but for the development of an understanding of harmony and led to improvising at the piano. 'Her scales surged up and down like the waves of the sea, ebbing and flowing in magnificent harmonies as they moved from one key to another' (E27). This is how her daughter Eugenie would later describe Clara's warming-up routine.

Exercises to strengthen her fingers and to develop a sense of independence, confidence and accuracy and of the distance between notes meant that Clara soon excelled at sight-reading from music. She seldom needed to look at the keyboard and could concentrate entirely on piano music. Wieck was using technical studies to train her ear and her rhythmic accuracy simultaneously. He had special exercises to increase the stretch of her hands so that she was later able 'to play tenths with a free wrist action' (E118), and had no difficulty with the compass of large chords and wide-ranging passage-work. In later years she would include these in her own compositions, such as the Scherzo, Op 10.

A central point of Wieck's method, besides training her hands, was to develop a beautiful tone in her playing. In his essay 'Piano and Singing', Wieck demanded of his pupils that melody and phrasing should sing with an immaculate legato. Frédéric Chopin was another teacher who advised his pupils to listen to the best singers. Louis Spohr would admire the twelve-year-old Clara's 'magnificent legato touch' that elicited a more beautiful sound 'from the instruments themselves' when she played (F39). Wieck obtained this effect through a loose wrist and elbow action and extreme economy of movement, so that the beautiful round sound, rich with overtones, was not distorted by any tension. For him the most important aspects were 'beautiful performance', 'playing with feeling' and 'musical interpretation', even during study, rather than the 'mechanical fingerwork' of the virtuoso. Clara was therefore not to 'practise her music to death' (L1,9f). He established a similar schedule for academic learning: she attended school a few hours a day for just a year and a half. In the first year of her marriage she lamented her *ignorance of the sciences* and her *lack of reading* compared to her husband Robert (Tb111).

When she was seven, tutors were engaged to teach her French and English, that she would need for her future international career. Her musical education was wide-ranging: the Kantor at the Thomaskirche, Christian Theodor Weinlich, taught her theory of music and counterpoint, and the Director of the Leipzig Opera, Heinrich Dorn, gave her lessons in composition. Wieck also made use of the excellent teachers in the cities to which they toured: Siegfried Dehn for counterpoint in Berlin, the Hofkapellmeister, Carl Reissiger, for orchestration in Dresden, and for singing, the famous Johann Aloys Mieksch, who also taught Wilhelmine Schröder-Devrient and Agnese Schebest. Even violin-playing and score-reading was part of Wieck's holistic method.

Wieck was well aware, however, that a piano virtuoso 'would only be able to earn his bread and butter if he also gave lessons' (L1,23). In 1829 Clara was therefore allowed to teach her brother Alwin, who was two years her junior. From the age of six Clara regularly attended concerts at the Gewandhaus with her father, as well as the theatre and the opera. There was hardly an opera that she had not seen in Leipzig during the years that followed. Clara was not permitted to practise the piano for more than three hours a day. Her health and her physical development were also important: even as a child she had to keep up with her parents on walks lasting several hours. For the whole of her life she believed in long walks like these – surely one of the most important reasons for her almost inexhaustible strength and staying-power.

Parallel with his plans for her musical education, far from mere technical drilling, Wieck was preparing with equal care and forethought for Clara's concert career. Here she would need a suitable repertoire for her age. At ten she was working on the Piano Concerto in G major, Op 73, by Johann Nepomuk Hummel and the Concerto in E flat major (K271) by W A Mozart, as well as the Second Concerto by John Field. In addition, she needed a range of pieces 'ready in case she needed them' (T1,42), such as works for duet or solo piano by Hummel, Friedrich Kalkbrenner, Franz Hünten, Carl Czerny and Ludwig van Beethoven, and studies by Ignaz Moscheles and Johann Baptist Cramer. Wieck's choice here was of predominantly tuneful, brilliant virtuoso works, familiar in the contemporary repertoire. Clara had to be ready at the drop of a hat to impress famous musicians, or anyone of importance who was visiting Leipzig.

Wieck used his own house to further Clara's career as a concert pianist. They now lived in the Grimmaische Strasse. Wieck had become a highly-regarded businessman and teacher, and his house was a meeting place for the musical world of Leipzig. The music publishers Friedrich Hofmeister and Heinrich Probst were regular guests, as were the composer Heinrich Marschner, the influential doctor and music-lover Dr Ernst August Carus, and the editor of the *Allgemeine Musikalische Zeitung,* Gottfried Fink. There was scarcely a composer or musician who would not call on Wieck when in Leipzig. He would regularly put on small concerts or musical entertainments in the evening, ever the genial host, and his daughter would then be able to practise in private for her public performances. Naturally she was invited to other private gatherings as well, such as the musical evenings hosted by Dr Carus, where as a nine-year-old she played the Trio Op 96 by Hummel with professional musicians, and was 'less deficient' than 'the gentlemen who accompanied her' (L1,13). It was probably in this house that she met Robert Schumann for the first time.

Wieck took endless trouble to meet famous artists such as Niccolò Paganini, to hear them play and to introduce Clara to them. When he learned, quite by chance, that Paganini would be in Leipzig for just a short time, he hurried to meet him and tried to arrange a concert for him, though this idea foundered due to lack of interest on the part of the concert managers. He followed him to Berlin, listened to him in rehearsal and at concerts, made his acquaintance and was deeply impressed by qualities he himself most admired: the ease of his playing despite great technical difficulties, his lovely singing tone, and his versatility in different genres. When Paganini finally came to Leipzig for four concerts in October 1829, Wieck went to see him, with Clara, on the day before the first concert. Wieck had thought carefully about what she should play for Paganini: a Rondo for piano duet by Carl Krägen on a theme by Paganini, performed with her father, and her own Polonaise in E flat major. Commenting on her composition, Paganini said that she 'had an artistic career ahead of her, since she had sensitivity' (L1,17). The reason why Wieck encouraged his daughter to compose at such a young age was not only to fulfil his concept of her education – it was also part of the virtuoso's career to perform his or her own works. Clara lacked nothing in her professionalism – and Wieck could feel encouraged by Paganini's opinion.

By now Clara was well known in the musical circles of Leipzig, and had gained experience of performing in private, so Wieck made the first cautious steps for her appearance in public. Clara would not give a concert on her own, but would appear at an official Gewandhaus concert on 20 October 1828. She was nine years old, and just played a duet with Wieck's pupil Emilie Reichhold; nevertheless, she received much praise both from critics and from the audience. Before the concert she had to surmount the first test of her nerves: by mistake she was picked up

Clara Wieck in 1827. Ivory miniature by an unknown artist. During this year she was already writing short pieces and exercises of her own as well as studying the Piano Concerto in G major, Op 73, by Hummel and the Concerto in E flat major by Mozart.

by the wrong carriage and taken in quite another direction before the lovely glass coach from the Gewandhaus came to collect her. Her father was waiting for her at the concert hall, and she arrived in floods of tears. In order to calm his daughter, who was thoroughly upset, Wieck used psychology to turn this disaster into quite a normal occurrence: 'I quite forgot to tell you, Clärchen, that people are usually taken to the wrong place when they perform in public for the first time' (L1,15).

Encouraged by the results of Clara's first public performance, and by the praise from Paganini, Wieck risked the next step: that of presenting Clara in another city. In March 1830 they travelled to Dresden. He knew that Privy Counsellor Carl Gustav Carus would help him with introductions to court and nobility. Wieck made no secret of what he was hoping to gain from the month they would spend in Dresden: 'From here onwards Clara is to become famous and make a name for herself' in order 'to create an entrée to other courts'. She appeared before discerning music-lovers and 'in the most distinguished houses', and everyone was amazed at her 'musical development (not just as a virtuoso). No one could believe that she composed because no young woman of her age had done so before. And when she improvised on a given theme, everyone was ecstatic.' Wieck took care of all the arrangements. When the news came 'that Clara might well be invited to play at court', he ordered 'a new pink silk dress for 12 talers'. By this time Clara was already an experienced performer: 'she is incredibly bold when she is playing – the greater the company, the better she plays'. She thrived on the attention she received, even 'being smothered with kisses – she looks better than ever' (F25ff).

It was not the first time that Clara had been in Dresden, as she had played for smaller private gatherings. Perhaps she had to become familiar with the place Wieck had selected for her to make her name outside Leipzig, perhaps he was preparing her for her first appearance at the Gewandhaus. It was also his honeymoon – on 3 July 1828, four years after his divorce, Wieck had married Clementine Fechner, daughter of the pastor Samuel Traugott Fechner. She was not a musician, nor had she any ambitions of her own, but she clearly had a placid enough nature to balance

Wieck's impetuous and decisive character. They had three children, two of whom died young. Marie, who was born in 1832, was taught by Wieck, as Clara had been.

Clara never had a close relationship with her stepmother. She was a lively child who demanded her father's entire attention. Her 'restless temperament' (T1,6) was apparent in her piano playing too, since Paganini advised her 'not to play too restlessly, and with so much movement of her body' (T1,47). 'However wild she was', she still knew how to behave with 'the most admirable tact' when she was in distinguished company (F27). She was particularly fond of little kittens – she loved to pet them and play games with them.

As a child Clara remained preternaturally lively, despite her father's strict insistence on obedience and discipline and despite her early separation from her mother. A few days after her first appearance at the Gewandhaus, when Clara greatly needed to unwind, Wieck scolded her for being 'lazy, careless, untidy, pig-headed and disobedient' (L1,16) – maybe he wanted to prevent success going to her head – and he tore her music to shreds in front of her, but she knew that the storm would pass as its predecessors had done. A few days later he started her lessons again: he was not going to waste all the intelligence and teaching talent he had expended thus far on launching her career as a pianist. After their success in Dresden he was 'firmly convinced' that he should concentrate even harder on this and 'give his work its finishing touches' (F27).

On 8 November 1830, at half past six in the evening, Clara Wieck appeared at the Leipzig Gewandhaus for the first time in a concert that she herself was promoting. This marked the official launch of a concert career, that would end 61 years later in Frankfurt. On this occasion the programme was: Rondo Brillant for Piano and Orchestra, Op 101, by Friedrich Kalkbrenner, Variations brillants, Op 23, by Henri Herz, a Quartet, Op 230

The concert hall in the Leipzig Gewandhaus. Clara Schumann appeared here as a soloist on 74 occasions.

by Czerny, a Romance for Physharmonica [a sort of harmonium] and Piano performed with Friedrich Wieck, and some variations of her own. Her performance and her compositions were much admired and 'earned her the greatest applause' (L1,25).

Even the Christmas holidays could not be devoted to family celebrations, but were used for the beginning of a concert tour: five weeks in Dresden from 24 December. It was here that Wieck pushed his daughter into competition for fame and popularity with the most famous female pianists of the day, Anna Caroline de Belleville and Leopoldine Blahetka, and later with Camille Pleyel – Wieck had been following their development very carefully. It was also the first time they had come up against the realities of touring life: following two successful concerts, they were refused the use of one hall in Dresden, only out of envy and spite. Similar things were to happen to them on their second concert tour, when they stopped in Weimar, Erfurt, Kassel,

Gotha, Arnstadt, Frankfurt, and Darmstadt, between late September 1831 and the middle of February 1832, on their way to Paris. In Kassel the 'jealousy of the theatrical world' was so great that posters were not displayed (T2,156); in Weimar, Wieck could not even count on Hummel's patronage, although Clara had always played his works with great success; when they first tried to visit Goethe in Weimar the Oberhofmarschall von Spiegel brushed them off, and denied them use of the theatre. But Wieck did not give up so easily. Through the good offices of new and like-minded combatants, on 1 October they had the first of two meetings with Goethe, who was eighty-three by this time. His comments: 'Clara's interpretation makes one see beyond the composition' (works by Herz), and 'the girl has more power than six boys put together' (he was surely not just referring to physical strength), were valuable recommendations. Thereafter Clara and Wieck were even invited to court by the Oberhofmarschall himself (L1,29).

Clara often had to battle with poor instruments. She was obliged to perform 'on a miserable crate' (T1,78) or a 'rattling box' or on something 'that could only be called "a dreadful heap of wood"' (T2,116). In Arnstadt Wieck refused to let her perform 'on a piano with a black keyboard, where the short keys were too narrow' (T2,128). Wieck was at his wits' end in Paris when he wondered whether Clara 'should adapt her playing in order to perform on the dry set of bones available locally, that prevents any fine shading or intelligent interpretation' (T2,203). And in Kassel he complained about how seldom Clara had the chance 'to find a good grand piano on which she can really show how she can play' (T2,144). In the letters he wrote to arrange concerts and recommendations for her, he laid particular emphasis on the fact that he had 'taught Clara in the splendid school of Field'. By this he meant in particular the nuances of colour and touch, a singing legato, a technique of fluently phrasing fast passages, and most definitely not the 'purely mechanical, monotonous Viennese style of Hummel' (T2,112). Wieck called her a 'musical pianist' (T2,124), who 'can offer something more than mere mechanical dexterity' (T2,102).

Critics and reference writers of the time did indeed confirm that Wieck's teaching methods had not just developed Clara's talent as a pianist. Professor Mensing in Erfurt was 'convinced that she is already the best pianist and that she will soon leave all other players far behind . . . she is destined to raise music itself to new levels of the sublime' (L1,31ff). Spohr recommended that 'her playing differs from that of the usual precocious virtuoso, not just as a result of strict and exemplary teaching, but also because of her natural gifts . . .' (L1,37). The *Gothaische Zeitung* wrote: 'Clara Wieck is no hot-house flower, there is nothing forced about her; her extraordinary virtuosity is rather an early manifestation of her innate musical genius' (L1,34). In 1832 the *Allgemeine Musikalische Zeitung* spoke of her great 'accomplishment, confidence and strength', but found that 'the depth of understanding and feeling in her playing' was even more remarkable (R47); and in the *Komet* there was a comparison with de Belleville written by Robert Schumann: 'Clara's tone finds its way to the heart and speaks to the soul. The one is poetic, but the other is poetry itself' (L1,52). From the way Clara was already playing at the time, and Wieck teaching, the performing style of most virtuosos must have appeared cold and unfeeling to them both.

However, alongside Wieck's pleased and proud reports of Clara's success, such as the one from Weimar where she was regarded as *'the Forever Unforgettable'*, (F36), there was a different message from Erfurt, where 'no one was capable of understanding Clara's playing' (T2,102). In Frankfurt, where that January it was bitterly cold and unwelcoming, and both of them were 'thoroughly' frozen in their large room, Wieck wrote sadly in the diary: 'no one takes the slightest notice of us – no one wants to hear Clara play' (T2,178). And although Clara played better than ever before when a concert finally took place in the auditorium at the museum, Wieck was disgusted at 'how cold and unfeeling' the audience had been. 'May God preserve all musicians from Frankfurt' (T2,188). It also became clear to Wieck in Kassel that Clara's age – she was twelve at the time – was not necessarily an advantage, 'since everyone avoids the so-called prodigies, who have usually had a few pieces drummed into them, but who are not musical' (F39).

It is true, at that time the concert halls were over-run with a plague of 'hot-house virtuosos' and 'miniature girl prodigies', as the critics called them. They were met with rejection and indifference, though they were found fascinating if they appeared to play sublimely while still looking like small children. Wieck therefore had to do some quick thinking about programme strategy while Clara was performing in private circles, in order to get permission for an appearance at the opera or theatre. 'First impressions mean a lot'. What should she play in order to 'demonstrate all aspects of her talent'? Should it be her own compositions, or works by Herz, Field or Johann Peter Pixis? Or should she simply improvise? She was aware that she had to 'make the best impression with a single piece' (L1,35). And her personal appearance was important too. Gifts of beautiful clothes were welcomed, and income from concerts was invested in Clara's wardrobe. She was therefore particularly angry when spiders at the 'pigsty guesthouse' in Weimar damaged her expensive silk dress because it 'hung the wrong way out' (F35).

This 'spider friendly guesthouse' was not an isolated incident. The accommodation they were offered was often damp and cold as well as dirty, or they were 'roughly treated' and 'swindled' (T2,92). Meals were 'very expensive', and the rooms were 'dark', and certainly made them feel depressed. Wieck found bad meals and unmannerly service, 'with a dirty knife and tin spoon', quite unbearable; even 'the most wonderful mattresses' were a poor recompense (T2,149). In future he intended to avoid small places and middle-sized towns 'if one does not wish to feel hurt, unrecognised and undervalued' (T2,106). Concerts in these places did not pay either for a man who was keeping exact accounts of income and outgoings: 'The expenses are too great for such a low ticket price – they are not sufficiently receptive, too cold, the accompaniment bad and imprecise – too few connoisseurs – life in the inns poor and expensive – then such monstrous trouble with the pianos, even to get them tuned' (T3,61).

Clara must have been extraordinarily resilient as a child in order to withstand these innumerable problems. It is remarkable that in these circumstances she seldom played 'in a cold, distracted and disinterested fashion', or neglected to cover when 'in the tuttis the orchestra made a mistake, or missed their entry' – as she was expected to do (this would happen mostly in small places). She even had to cope with noise and disturbance even during her performance. In Arnstadt the noise of tea being served and general moving around distracted her so much that she lost her concentration in a cadenza. Later in her career she would react strongly to such bad manners, and simply stop playing.

Small wonder that after four months of touring around Germany Wieck made no secret of how 'fed up' he was 'with travelling' (F42). But they still had to make the journey to Paris, starting from Bibrich in a post-coach that was meant for four but had been 'stuffed' with six people. They travelled for four days and four nights, arriving in Paris on the evening of 15 February 1832. Wieck had no need to worry about how Clara would withstand the cold: she had 'weathered everything like a Russian' (F44).

Wieck had arranged their stay in Paris through the painter Eduard Fechner, his wife's brother, who lived in the city. His poor knowledge of the French language caused him as many problems as his ignorance of the different customs. In Paris smoking was only permitted in their room, which was bitterly cold with its stone floor and 'miserable fireplace'. Clara always had to wear white, and a different dress for each soirée, although they only had a 'tumblerful of water' to wash with each day (F44ff). Clara, aged twelve, found these soirées particularly difficult as in Paris they began at ten in the evening, lasting

The Place de la Bourse, Paris. Painting by Giuseppe Canella, 1830. Friedrich Wieck made his first foreign tour with Clara to Paris in 1832.

until one, and were quite foreign to her in their stiff artificiality. Nevertheless, she could gain attention here, and she even won over Kalkbrenner, who was present.

These private performances, where Clara played her Scherzi and Variations, as well as compositions by Pixis and Herz, and improvisations, were designed to prepare the way for a public concert. The first of these took place on 9 April, in modest circumstances since an outbreak of cholera had driven people out of Paris. Clara played from memory – an extra strain – but this was customary in Paris. Performance without music, unknown in Germany at the time, would be construed in an absurd way later: that she could only play by looking at the keys. Bettina von Arnim condemned playing from memory as pretentious and a way of showing off (L1,107).

They spent two and a half months in Paris, returning to Leipzig on 1 May 1832. While this visit had not fulfilled all Wieck's hopes, they did make useful contacts for the future with Giacomo Meyerbeer, Ferdinando Paer, Georges Onslow and most importantly with Ferdinand Hiller, Frédéric Chopin, Franz Liszt and Felix Mendelssohn Bartholdy, all of whom would become friends or acquaintances. And Wieck was able to gauge how Clara stood in comparison to other pianists. He avoided open competition because he was aware that a pianist like the Austrian Blahetka, who was eight years older, would have more connections to call on than Clara, especially with Kalkbrenner. When he heard what Herz was playing, however, he was able to confirm Clara's superiority and that of his own methods: 'Indeed, he plays without heart, the hands jump without any soul.' (T2,212) He was well aware that neither presentation nor hand movements communicated the meaning and expression of the music.

Frédéric Chopin. Portrait circa 1831 by unknown artist. In 1831 Clara Wieck, then aged 12, introduced in Germany his virtuoso Variations, Op 2, on Là ci darem la mano, that were published in 1830.

The most important contact to make in Paris was with Chopin. The previous year

Clara had mastered his Variations on 'Là ci darem la mano', Op 2, in the space of just one week, and found *this is the most difficult piece of music I have ever seen and played. This original and witty composition is still so little-known that almost all pianists and teachers consider it unplayable and incomprehensible* (T2,73). She had caused a sensation with these variations in Weimar. Wieck's opinion of the E minor Concerto, when he heard it in Paris, might apply just as well to these variations: 'It is quite in the style of Field, and if I did not know the composer I would have thought it was the work of Schumann.' He also wrote that the passage work was new, 'incredibly difficult and brilliant in an unusual way' (T2,212). The new passages were wide-ranging not small-scale, extending the melodic lines with fluency and energy, and were quite unlike the conventional virtuosity and brilliance of Pixis, Hummel, Kalkbrenner or Herz. Wieck wrote a review of the variations that was intended for the Paris 'Revue Musicale', calling them a 'Fantasia'. Chopin, on the other hand, was not at all enamoured of this text and was able to prevent publication through the intervention of Hiller. Wieck had therefore achieved the opposite of what he had intended: Chopin was elusive in Paris rather than benevolent.

Meanwhile two of Clara Wieck's own compositions had appeared: the *Quatre Polonaises pour le Pianoforte*, Op 1, and the *Caprices en forme de valse pour le piano*, Op 2. The first of these polonaises – presumably the piece that she had played to Paganini in 1829 – demonstrates how the ten-year-old composer could already handle the combination of different moods. In the trio of the *Ländler* she contrasts vigorous leaps of fourths in the bass, and motifs developed from sweeping and wide-ranging figures, against a gentle progression of double stops and chromatic melodies that seem to circle within themselves. The bold leaps and appoggiaturas of the third polonaise are followed by the free-flowing melody of a sensitive and expressive trio. The staccati of the trio to the fourth polonaise, where the left hand is more than mere accompaniment, foreshadow those spine-chilling ghost stories so typical of the Romantic Epoch.

The nine *Caprices* – apparently written before and during the concert tour – are full of witty ideas. Although they are written in waltz time they are character pieces, or, as Schumann called them 'more like impromptus, or Wieck's "Moments musicales" (L1,48). They are full of surprising harmonic turns, that change the character of the composition, immediately enriching its contrasts of mood and dynamics, where the young composer is using a wide range of pianistic expressions, such as repeated notes for their terse rhythms (No 8), or their melodic sensitivity (No 6). These pieces are more than echoes of Schumann's *Papillons*, Op 2. Interest lies rather in the effects Clara Wieck was seeking to achieve in her harmony, and how much she was using this as a means of expression as well as of colour. She creates form and mood with originality, for instance, in the second Caprice: this opens with what might be called harmony on the up-beat, using the chord of the dominant seventh, so that the simple little melody seems to hover. Then she allows the piece to gently die away with the same chord; only two lightly struck bass notes lead back to the tonic.

The *Romance variée pour le Piano*, Op 3, was also composed in about 1831. When the variations were published in 1833 Clara dedicated the work to Schumann: *The inspired way in which you will rework this little musical thought has to make up for my poor work, and so I request you to do that, since I can hardly wait to get to know it better.* Schumann, however, was obviously having trouble in completing his *Impromptus sur une Romance de Clara Wieck*, Op 5, based on the theme from her Op 3. He lamented that 'for a long time any progress was subsequently crossed out' (L1,64ff). Clara had written variations in the Romantic style, using virtuoso piano techniques to develop the theme with different tones and colours.

Leipzig. A view of the marketplace from the Waage. Copper engraving with water colour, 1820, by an unknown artist.

They are very lively and are framed by a slow introduction where the theme is freely quoted and by a stretta that brings the work to its dynamic climax most effectively.

The seven months of touring clearly left its mark. Back in Leipzig, an entry in the diary reads: Clara should 'no longer play and study gallant pieces' since 'she cannot practice and play slowly any more' (T2,241). From 1832 onwards her repertoire is quite different. It still contained works by contemporary composers such as Sigismund Thalberg, Pixis or Adolph Henselt, but now the emphasis was on Beethoven, Bach, Chopin, Schumann and Mendelssohn. Wieck understood his audiences, and knew how to make pleasing combinations of the new and the conventional: if Clara were to play a Bach fugue, Beethoven's 'Appassionata' and a mazurka by Chopin at a concert in Plauen, then the audience would be 'cold'; only 'Herz's Op 36 would warm them up again' (T4,175ff). There was also a difference between a public concert and a private recital: at the first the public had to be courted, at the second unknown works could be introduced – not least, those by Schumann. In addition to this different repertoire there were new, intensive studies to be made, and lessons in composition and counterpoint with Heinrich Dorn. Wieck had sent Schumann, then aged twenty-one, to Dorn the previous year, but Schumann only just completed one year of tuition on fugue.

There were two concert-free months after they returned from Paris, but Clara then gave three performances in the Gewandhaus. On 9 July 1832, in a programme devised using the new strategy, she played Chopin's Op 2, with works by Pixis and Herz on either side. Wieck did not stick to his principle of not letting Clara perform in small towns. For someone who had worked his way up from deepest poverty, these offers, with their earning potential, were too advantageous to turn down. Clara's career had also meant that he had had to give up his music lending business. Between 1832 and 1837 he and Clara made eight small concert tours to nearby areas. In November 1832 they visited Altenburg, Zwickau and Schneeberg. Clara had to recuperate from scarlet fever after this tour, but in January 1833 she was already back playing in Leipzig: on 10 January at a subscription concert, and on the morning of 13 January at a musical event organised by her father, where she probably played her Caprices, Op 2, for the first time. It is amazing how often Clara performed in Leipzig between the ages of thirteen and eighteen. There were approximately twenty concerts, each with a different programme, to say nothing of the private recitals.

The loss of her half-brother Clemenz, *my dearest darling*, at the beginning of 1833, was a severe blow to Clara. He died suddenly at just three years old (T3,3). Instead of giving a concert as planned in Leipzig two days after her brother's death, she set off the very next day with her father for Dresden, *to alleviate the pain* (T3,4). In later years she would always seek to overcome mental anguish with activity, travel or performance.

In July of that year Clara made the acquaintance of Emilie

List, the fifteen-year-old daughter of the economist Friedrich List, who had returned to Germany as an American consul, and settled in Leipzig in 1833 to promote the idea of a German railway network. Clara had no contact with girls of her own age, as it was a long time since she had attended school. Emilie, who had travelled widely, had a liberal upbringing, and had much greater experience of life and linguistic fluency than Clara, became her first and lifelong friend. She confided her joys and sorrows to Emilie in almost 300 letters.

Clara herself must have made a strong impression as well. In her home surroundings she appeared 'ingenuous and childlike' and it was only when observed more closely that another side appeared: 'The pretty face with its fine features, the slightly strange angle to the eyes, the kind-looking mouth with its sensitive expression, occasionally mocking or showing pain' gave the impression 'that the child could tell a long story, a mixture of joy and pain, but – what does she know about? – music' (L1,67ff). Five years later she would write to Schumann: *You will give me back the years of my youth; I was always such a stranger in the world, my father loved me very much, as I loved him, but I never enjoyed a mother's love, so necessary for a girl, and so I was never completely happy* (S575).

Clara Wieck. Oil painting by an unknown artist, circa 1835/36.

It was also in July that Clara began to study the recently

published Piano Concerto in E minor by Chopin. On 29 September she was the first to perform the finale of this concerto in Leipzig. On 7 February 1834 Wieck and his daughter again set off on a small concert tour to Altenburg, Gera and Plauen that lasted until 14 April. Then on 11 November they embarked on a five-month tour of northern Germany, to Halle, Magdeburg, Brunswick, Hanover, Bremen, Hamburg and Berlin, returning home 18 April 1835. Clara performed regularly until August, when she *composed and orchestrated her waltzes*, that were performed shortly afterwards *in the Kuchengarten and the Hotel de Prusse with success* (W55). Her *Valses romantiques pour le Piano*, Op 4, are only preserved in their piano version. In this playful set of waltzes, closely related to each other but in a free arrangement, each piece has an individual character. The first waltz, after a few quiet bars of introduction, immediately establishes the effusive and optimistic tone of the work.

When Chopin visited Leipzig in September he paid a call on Wieck, despite, or maybe because of, the misunderstanding in Paris, and waited patiently for an hour until Clara appeared. She played Schumann's Sonata in F sharp minor as well as part of her concerto, whereupon he *showered her with compliments* (T4,161). Almost a year later, on 12 September 1836, she played three of her compositions to him, Ops 5, 6 and 7.

He was so enthusiastic about her *Quatre Pièces caractéristiques*, Op 5, that he took them away with him immediately. Small wonder: the four pieces are thoroughly Romantic mood pictures: the first, *Le Sabbat* is fast and furious, with shifted accents, and the terse rhythmic figure of two semiquavers and one quaver that Clara uses repeatedly, even inverted, as in the fourth piece. The insistent repetitive notes of the second piece, *Caprice à la Boléro* are fidgety and rhythmically strong – another pianistic device that Clara used frequently – with a lyrical central section; the *Romance* is dreamy with a polyphonic melodic pattern. The tritone leaps in the bass of the fourth piece, *Scène fantastique*, the ballet of the ghosts, are reminiscent of the fourths in the first Polonaise, Op 1. Her ghostly characters are introduced in various musical scenarios, until in the silently fading ending they leave the theatre like vanishing spectres.

Clara had played the two mazurkas and the ballade from her *Soirées Musicales*, Op 6, to Chopin on purpose; she was hoping for his opinion on the music with which he was very familiar. Her 'Notturno' contained excited, dynamic outbursts, like Chopin's own nocturnes, going well beyond the gentle calm of night. Schumann would later write that he found it melancholy and 'his favourite', and add: 'then the trio to the Toccatina' (S100), by which he was referring to its central section, the yearning song in the first of these six pieces. In 1838 Liszt would play the Op 6 'at sight' (T6,85).

Clara also played the whole of her Concerto for Piano and Orchestra in A minor, Op 7, to Chopin. She had begun composition of the final movement three years earlier, in January 1833, finished it in December, and given it to Schumann who *wants to orchestrate it now* (T3,47). In this she, the much better-known musician, was showing great trust in the capabilities of a composer who was still unknown and only taking his first steps in orchestral music. She only orchestrated the first movement herself. It was written in 1834 and was to be her only work for orchestra; she wrote the second movement *where the adagio in the middle is only with a cello obligato*, the following year (W55).

The first performance was conducted by Mendelssohn on 9 November 1835. Critical opinion was kind but not enthusiastic. It would seem that Clara reworked this concerto before its publication in 1837, and she played it later to great acclaim in Vienna. It is a work full of drive and energy, that goes beyond the formal conventions of the past to create an impression of originality and cohesion both in the language of the music and in its construction. The rising theme of the first movement, with its onward drive, is recast in the poetic idiom of the Romance, and developed in the final movement into a lively motif with a dance-like rhythm. Then, just when the tension of the melodic lines seems overbearing, it is released in figurations like free fantasies that carry the music forward. The transitions between the three linked movements point to changes in their character, but do not detract from the element of surprise.

More than two years were to elapse before Wieck again set out with Clara on a tour of north Germany on 7 February 1837. Clara, now eighteen, had been working on her new *Variations de Concert pour le Piano-Forte*, Op 8, in order to take it on this tour. This is a brilliant and technically challenging bravura piece *Sur la Cavatine du Pirate de Bellini* (On a cavatina from Bellini's opera 'Il pirata') – the arrangement of melodies from Italian operas was a popular genre of the time. Clara's individual style can be seen in the unexpected changes of mood and her impetuosity. She had to play the variations several times to Gaspare Spontini in Berlin because *they delighted him every time* (T6,100). Clara made a great impression also with Bach and Beethoven at her first soirée in Berlin. It was only Ludwig Rellstab (who had also fulminated against Chopin) who considered Clara's playing *monotonous* (T6,23). Rellstab passed no judgement on her own compositions and was of the magnanimous opinion that 'in a few years she will learn to play melodies better' (T6,92). He would also make life difficult for her in Berlin at a later date; *this boor who considers himself a critic*, she wrote angrily when he simply overlooked Schumann's second sonata in 1840 (T9,142).

No sooner had she reached the Hotel de Russie on 8 February than Clara was impatient to see her mother again. She visited Marianne Bargiel *and everything was better than I expected* (T6,83). It was not long before the old animosity between her father and his first wife flared up again – *Madame B began to poke her nose into my concert arrangements* (T6,99) – and it is probable that this spoiled their reunion after so many years of separation.

Clara's impressions after first meeting Bettina von Arnim were ambivalent. At first she thought she was a *highly intelligent, excitable woman – as far as music is concerned, her opinions are all wrong* (T6,86) – but she was very good-humoured. Then later, when Bettina von Arnim, speaking to a third person, had called Clara *the most disagreeable artist I have ever met*, the younger woman quickly revised her judgement to a thoroughly *mad woman!* (T6,93).

After the strain of eight performances in Berlin – 'of playing against a background of such animosity, lying, slander and deceit' (T6,99) – they went on to Hamburg, where Clara had a rapturous reception from her second concert onwards, although even here there was mention of *a reviewer like a rhinoceros* (T6,108). After the third concert in Hamburg she played her difficult Op 8 at a concert in Bremen with flickering gas lighting. Back in Leipzig – on 3 May 1837 – she looked at the works by Liszt that had just appeared – *new and original* (T6,118). She spent the summer in Dresden and at Maxen, as a guest of Major Serre, and played through piles of operas and orchestral works with Carl Krägen. In August her father fetched her back, because he had announced her appearance in Leipzig: *Like it or not – I have to do it!* – (T6,133). She had her greatest success hitherto in the Leipzig Gewandhaus on 8 October with a work of customary brilliance: Henselt's Variations on Donizettis 'Elisir d'Amore'. And that was just a week before she set off for Vienna, where she would have her greatest triumph as a pianist so far, despite all the mental anguish.

A Double Life

Robert Schumann was born on 8 June 1810 in Zwickau, the son of August Schumann, publisher, bookseller and writer, and his wife Johanne Christiane, née Schnabel. In 1828, while Schumann was studying law in Leipzig at his mother's behest, he decided to take piano lessons with Wieck. His father had died two years previously, and with him Schumann had lost any support for his musical and literary aspirations. He did not, however, remain in Leipzig for long – he continued his law studies in Heidelberg. From there he travelled to Italy before returning to Leipzig in 1830. He had finally decided on a career in music. His mother, troubled by her son's change of heart, turned to Wieck asking whether it was worth Robert 'starting again at the beginning' after 'three wasted years' (R62). Wieck replied conscientiously that he would undertake to 'make Robert into one of the greatest living pianists, given his talent and his imagination', but this would require an extremely disciplined working schedule, and he doubted whether 'charming' Robert, who as a student in Heidelberg had drunk and smoked a lot and not lived in an exactly frugal manner, would 'now change and develop greater concentration, application and strength of mind' (L1,21).

In the autumn of 1830 Robert Schumann, now aged twenty, moved into two rooms in Wieck's house where he stayed until the end of 1832. He worked with Wieck in the mornings, if he was not away touring with Clara. The afternoon was for walking. 'The best time was in the evening. Then Robert took the children, Clara and her two brothers Alwin and Gustav, to his room and became a child again with them. He told them fables he invented himself, made up charades for them, and created stories for Clara, who was rather frightened, about Doppelgänger, and his pistol . . . she always believed him implicitly . . . You can well imagine how much she must have loved him' (ES223f).

Robert's relationship with Wieck at this time was ambivalent. He respected and admired him, dedicating his Op 5 to him, and he even missed him when Wieck went on tour with Clara, but at the same time he called him 'Mr. Moneybags' and described him as 'dull, boring and arrogant' (Ta371,389). At the same time Robert could see how easily Clara made progress; this led him to extremes in his own practising, with the result that his middle finger became stiff. Wieck's bad

Robert Schumann as a student in Leipzig. Reproduction of a missing portrait by an unknown artist, circa 1834.

temper also frightened Robert, who was gentle and quiet, rather introverted, and often silent in company. Wieck had, however, recognized Robert's talent from the outset. He valued his compositions so highly that he never prevented his daughter from performing them, even during the periods when he was keeping Clara and Schumann apart.

In April 1834 Ernestine von Fricken came to live in Wieck's house as his pupil. Clara had come to know this charming girl, three years her elder, shortly before this in Plauen. In May Clara was sent by her father to Dresden for music lessons, perhaps because he was already aware of her feelings for Robert. When she returned in September she had the impression that Ernestine and Robert were engaged. These rumours also reached the ears of Ernestine's father, who fetched his daughter home to Asch.

In her later correspondence with Robert Clara remembered this period with sadness. At the time she was hurt and cross – she did not miss Ernestine, who was rather like a plant that only thrives when it is watered, but *the sun was too hot for her – i.e. Herr Schumann* (T4,90). Robert did give Ernestine a ring as a farewell present, but they were never formally engaged. After he had paid a visit to Asch, where he learned that she was only the adopted daughter of Herrn von Fricken, with no claims to an inheritance, his enthusiasm began to cool. In April 1835 Clara returned from a tour of north Germany and made a deep impression on him: 'You seemed taller, different – you were no longer a child . . . Ernestine vanished as she had to do' (S96). What Clara felt on this tour can only be surmised from Wieck's words: 'Clara plays reluctantly, and does not really want to do anything' (L1,81).

Clara had fallen in love with Robert long before he recognised that she was becoming a woman. At that time he was a good-looking young man, with long brown hair and deep, expressive blue eyes, an elegant and noble appearance, a good-natured and engaging personality – Clara would often speak in later years of the gentle expression of his eyes. 'The first kiss in November' 1835 (Ta,421) marked the end of his attachment to Ernestine and the beginning of Clara and Robert's story, with all its ups and downs.

In February 1836, when Wieck learned that Robert had taken advantage of his own absence of several days to visit Clara in Dresden, he threatened in his blinding anger that he would shoot Robert if he should ever try to see her again. From then until August 1837, for a year and a half, Clara and Robert were prevented from either speaking or writing to one another. Their correspondence was resumed through the intervention of their mutual friend Ernst Adolf Becker, and through the concert on 13 August in the Börsensaal in Leipzig, where Clara played three of Robert's *Etudes symphoniques*. He was present at the concert, and thanked Wieck afterwards *for the pleasure it gave him* (L1,120). 14 August was regarded by them both as the day of their engagement. On 13 September, Clara's birthday, Robert wrote to Wieck asking for her hand in marriage, but he received no definite answer. Downcast and disheartened, he turned to Clara: 'you will have to be very strong; . . . he will coerce you if he cannot achieve his ends by cunning' (S24f). Clara would often have to dispel Robert's fears and doubts about her steadfastness, and not only towards her father, although it was usually he himself who upset her.

Wieck did not allow matters to disturb his preparations for a tour to Vienna. On 15 October 1837 he set off with Clara for Dresden, then Prague, where her two concerts brought *enormous satisfaction to the whole audience* (T6,155). They reached Vienna, their final destination, on 27 November. At eighteen Clara was no longer a prodigy who could trade on her age; now she was an artist who had to compete with the great performers Thalberg, Liszt and Chopin, although they were almost ten years older than she. The musical city of Vienna was her

Clara Wieck. Lithograph by Andreas Staub, 1838, at the time of her triumphant success in Vienna. Robert Schumann wrote to Clara about this picture and the artist in April 1839: 'I might be afraid of him, since he has seen so deep into your heart.'

greatest artistic and pianistic challenge to date, as she well knew.

Before her first concert the press announced the competition: 'Vienna shall decide whether she can be ranked alongside Thalberg' (T6,167), and although beforehand Clara had *filled everyone with enthusiasm*, she faced her first concert with *some trepidation* (S54). Then the debut, on 14 December, *the day that shall decide my fate* (S65). Afterwards she could report with pride: *My first concert in the hall of the Musikverein – my triumph . . . I was called back to the stage twelve times* (T6,171f). She played to the Empress, and after her second concert, on 27 December, when she 'had eighteen curtain calls and each time the applause was like thunder', she had become 'the talk of the town, and it is all the rage to have heard the one and only Clara' (T6,176f). After her third concert, on the evening of 7 January, in the city where, when she arrived 'Thalberg was every second word' (T6,167), the competition was finally over: 'Clara's complete victory over Thalberg' (T6,182). Wieck's rejoicing after the fourth Concert on 21 January was in even more military terms: 'The greatest of triumphs . . . Victory over the enemies' (T6,187).

Clara thought of herself as unremarkable, but on the (admittedly somewhat idealised) evidence of the lithograph made of her by Andreas Staub at that time in Vienna, she must have made a considerable impression on the stage. She was also a born performer, even when tired: *fed up with playing and yet, heaven knows, if I am playing in public I always play with the same enthusiasm* (S131). And she enjoyed her success: *No better feeling than to have pleased the whole audience* (S1,58). She not only stood up to the professional competition, it spurred her on. She even met organised opposition with a fighting spirit: *Tomorrow my opponents have decided to hiss at me, but I am a girl within my own armour* (L1,190). Even her critical father had to admit that when Clara was buoyed up by such a reception she outshone herself and rose to incredible heights.

She judged the taste for music in Vienna correctly and reaped the consequences: *They know everything by Chopin and understand him . . . Mendelssohn is almost unknown, his Songs without Words are unsold in the music shops – they don't sing here! . . . I wanted to play something by him at the first concert, but I did not dare until I had the audience on my side.* She was aware at what point she could offer the audience something unknown: *if the first impression here is a good one, then the artist can do whatever he likes* (S54f).

The programme strategies they had worked out went like this: at the first concert there was a judicious mixture of Pixis, Henselt and Chopin; at the second she risked her own piano concerto alongside Henselt and Chopin, and – unprecedented in Vienna – a Bach fugue, that she had to repeat, no less. The pattern continued: at the third concert she dared to perform for her Viennese audience her own Variations, Op 8, and Beethoven's Appassionata Sonata in F minor, Op 57. When, at the fourth concert, she continued the virtuoso

Franz Liszt. Painting by Jean Gabriel Scheffer, 1835/36. Clara's feelings about Liszt were ambivalent. She thought him a bad composer. On his death in 1886 she wrote 'he was an eminent piano virtuoso, but a dangerous example for the young. Almost all the rising players imitated him, but they lacked his imagination, his genius and his charm' (L3,479).

challenge, and played works by Liszt and Thalberg, criticism that she could not play Beethoven only increased the number of her supporters amongst – *those who had still thought that I couldn't play Thalberg* (S79). At the fifth concert she introduced Mendelssohn, with his Capriccio in B minor, Op 22, 'suitably accompanied by the orchestra', and generated such interest that he was 'now on the tip of everyone's tongue' and 'his opponents are silent' (F91). On 18 February, at her sixth and last concert, she played the Appassionata Sonata again, since in the meantime *battle* had broken out *in the newspapers* (T6,187), the *Clara war*, and *all over a sonata* (S88). It may have been her reading of this sonata that divided opinion; she certainly did not play it as a heroic piece, but rather brought out its expressive depths and the strength of its moods. For Franz Grillparzer she had found the key to this work, and he wrote a poem on the impression her performance had made on him. Liszt, who thought her a 'highly interesting pianist', admiring her 'technical mastery, and the depth and truth of her feelings, as well as her ever noble bearing', found that her interpretation of this sonata was 'remarkable and strangely beautiful' (L1,201). Yet it was Liszt himself who shook her confidence for a time: he played her *Soirées Musicales* at sight and so impressed her that she found her own playing to be insipid by comparison, and thought she looked *just like a schoolgirl* (S159).

She constructed her programmes with great skill and audience awareness. She did not win the hearts of the Viennese with salon pieces or superficial virtuosity; she did put in bravura pieces here and there, but the focal point was compositions of the romantic school – Chopin, Liszt and Mendelssohn. At that time it was very daring of her to include Bach and Beethoven. She did not play Robert Schumann's works publicly, fearing that they would be disliked and misunderstood, but at private recitals, where her sight-reading also received 'enormous admiration', she seldom neglected the opportunity to make his work known. Even Liszt was introduced to Schumann's *Carnaval* in this way (F76).

Despite all her concerts and performances, Clara also found time to compose her *'Souvenir de Vienne', Impromptu pour le Pianoforte,* Op 9. This work appeared in print for the first time in Vienna, as did her Op 8, and her compositions sold extremely well. Wieck was convinced: 'If Clara had time now she would compose many beautiful things' (F77). She performed the technically demanding Impromptu for the first time in Graz on 30 April 1838, 'to a furore' (T7,3). It contains variations on

Manuscript of Clara Wieck's *Souvenir de Vienne*, 1838. The composer wrote to Robert Schumann in April of that year: 'it is just a little impromptu, but it went down very well; you can appeal to the Austrians very much with their folk song' (S122).

Joseph Haydn's Imperial Hymn, moving between passages of great sensitivity and euphoric climaxes.

On 15 May 1838 father and daughter returned to Leipzig after a tour lasting seven months that had been extremely strenuous for both of them. Clara was suffering from strain in her arms and Wieck had facial pains. Each one of Clara's appearances must have racked his nerves. At the first concert the *storm of applause . . . reduced him to tears* (T6,172), so great had been the tension; before the third concert he 'passed a sleepless night', worrying how Clara was 'to do as well as she had done in the second concert' (F77). After her last performance he was quite decided: this was his last tour. He could no longer stand Clara's contradictory nature and self-assertion, the strain of promoting concerts, his fears and unease over his own health (F89). When Wieck no longer wished to travel with Clara to Paris it was not just primarily on account of their arguments over Robert.

Alongside her numerous obligations, including the social ones, Clara was leading a parallel life through her secret correspondence with Robert. These love letters are full of longing, emotion and endearments, but they also contain hints of difficulties to come. How had Robert, still unknown as a composer, although in the meantime the owner and editor of the *Neue Zeitschrift für Musik*, reacted to the reports of her success? They made him 'quite melancholy', since 'no one knows what your heart is feeling, no one knows me' (S69). When he heard a rumour that she was to be made a K K (Royal and Imperial) Kammervirtuosin, he referred to her numerous admiring 'love letters from young artists, male and female' (S101f). When Clara was indeed given this honour, although both a Protestant and a foreigner, she did not tell him, to spare his feelings. When he asked if it was always her choice to play her piano concerto – it had made 'no real impression' on him (S53) – she replied confidently: *Of course! I play it because everyone likes it . . . Whether it satisfies me personally, that is another question. Do you think me so weak that I don't know very well the shortcomings of this Concerto?* (S58).

During this period Schumann confided to her his traumatic experiences, his fears, his melancholy and depression. She must have known, even then, what these would lead to. His firm belief that she could 'heal him completely, make him thoroughly happy' (S74) and his announcement that she must be prepared for 'anxiety and suffering' (S147) were met by the eighteen-year-old Clara with the confidence of love and a trust in her own strength. But she was already worried about the future: would Robert's income suffice, would she *have to bury* her music although she was now enjoying her greatest success (S46)? It was she who made plans for the future, who suggested that he, at twenty-seven, should move to Vienna, since Wieck would never tolerate them living in Leipzig, so she would *not be able to earn a Dreyer with her art* (S109). There were also arguments, when she confessed how hurt she had been over Ernestine, and he asked her about her previous admirers. And his constant doubts: would her 'beautiful self-sacrificing love endure?' And would she be able to separate herself completely from her father? (S128)

Clara had decided on her secret engagement to Robert against the will of her father. Right up to her marriage, however, she would be beset by conflicting needs for an adult independence and her filial gratitude to her father, as well as those of anger and hurt. Between *yesterday he crowned it all with his rudeness – I am finished with him*, or, *if he weren't so useful to me here I would have sent him packing long ago* (S106), and *the separation from my father will be difficult for me* (S191), lie the shades of this emotional conflict.

Wieck's planning for Clara's career had been thoroughly vindicated in Vienna: the comprehensive musical education he had provided, his teaching methods, his career strategies had all withstood the acid test. Her enormous ability to deal with stress, her strength and the energy that would be required of her in later years, can be traced back to her father who may have asked much of her, but who always believed in her. The patronising manner in which Wieck wrote a diary in Clara's name, can also be regarded as symbiotic identification with Clara as the central point in his life, while his patriarchal, authoritarian attitude can be seen as a corset, that did indeed constrict her, but that also provided support. Wieck had written in Clara's diary when she was fourteen the advice that it was extremely important that she should now develop her independence and she should not let herself be upset by feelings of despondency when others misunderstood or envied her (L1,66).

Wieck had brought Clara up to be independent, to face life and to cope with it, and even in her younger years not to remain dependent on him. The many letters to musicians and to organisations, that he made her copy, did not just teach her to write; they were also lessons in the business of concert life. From Wieck's point of view, the thought of a union between Clara and

Robert, who could not guarantee a secure life for his daughter, and whose way of life so utterly contradicted his own idea of discipline, would have been intolerable. Wieck was afraid that this marriage would be the end of Clara's highly promising career, and the destruction of his life's work. It was for this reason that he remained firm and unyielding immediately after their return from Vienna. Nevertheless, Clara and Robert met secretly, often in curious circumstances: she would wave to Robert with a white handkerchief as he passed the window to indicate that she would meet him at the *old Neumarkt* (L1,215), and there was hardly a single 'ingress' or 'alley way' that the pair had not used (S202). Clara, who had to hide her feelings from Wieck at home, was less bothered by this game of hide and seek than Robert who felt 'so terribly sad, ill and upset' (L1,223).

MAD VIARDOT-GARCIA.

Shortly after her return, Clara made the acquaintance of the singer Pauline García, who was two years younger – *an interesting singer and certainly the most musical alive today*, in fact *a true artist* (T7,11).

Pauline Viardot-García. Lithograph by Pierre Vigneron, 1845. She was one of the famous singers that Clara Schumann accompanied. Others included Wilhelmine Schröder-Devrient, Jenny Lind and Julius Stockhausen.

Pauline Viardot-García (1821–1910), mezzo-soprano, composer and pianist. Daughter of the Spanish opera singer Manuel del Populo García, sister of Maria Malibran, the famous mezzo-soprano, and of Manuel Gracía, inventor of the laryngoscope, who also taught Jenny Lind and Julius Stockhausen. Married Louis Viardot, Director of the Théâtre Italien, Paris, in 1840. He was also her impresario.

Their close friendship was for life. We are 'the two oldest friends of the century' Pauline wrote to Clara in 1892.

Clara was composing again during the summer of 1838. She wrote her *Scherzo pour le Piano-Forte*, Op 10, at the Maxen estate near Dresden, although a letter from her father *hurt her* so much. The thought that he might perhaps disown her made her so ill that she could not sleep and her limbs shook (S191). This splendid piece with its breathless and vigorous theme is introduced by gently rocking and seeking trills that create a descending tonal space, that Clara also uses in inversion for the slower lamental sections. Then the opening figures and the theme are combined with varying harmonies and expressive forms until the piece ends elusively with falling broken chords. The Scherzo was published that same year by Breitkopf & Härtel, and was received with enormous enthusiasm in Paris: *It is odd that my scherzo is so popular here that I always have to repeat it* (S469).

In September 1838 Robert went to Vienna in the hope that he would be able to publish his magazine there. This would be necessary if he and Clara were to move to that city after their marriage and thus meet Wieck's condition for supporting themselves. Robert remained in Vienna until April 1839, but there was no prospect of financial security.

Clara gave several more concerts in Dresden and Leipzig during the autumn, then set off on 8 January 1839 on a tour she had been planning for a long time – a second visit to Paris, after an absence of seven years. She wanted to use Robert's absence in order to earn money herself, and also to further her own career by building on her success in Vienna. This time she had to travel without her mentor – *he would not come to Paris, and why not? Because he saw it as his duty to do nothing that might bring me nearer to my avowed aim. If he were to come with me he would be doing so, since I would be earning more* (S344). She could feel the downside of performing even in Nuremberg, but she was successful and did her accounting just as accurately as her father: *after the deduction of 41 Guilders in costs, an income of 191 Guilders and 21 Kreutzer* (T7,44). She travelled via Ansbach for another concert in Stuttgart, where she met Gustav Schilling, and was trusting enough to believe his generous promises to help her and Robert.

Robert knew that Schilling had a bad reputation, and for months he was a subject of conflict in their letters. Consciously or unconsciously she had aroused strong feelings of jealousy, 'like Othello's' (S409), since Robert, in Schilling's behaviour, saw simply a dishonest attempt to get closer to Clara, and he was correct in this view. His pride deeply wounded, Robert knew just how to hurt Clara, to exact 'revenge' (S391). At this point Clara realised that she had lost her father, or at any rate *her heart* was *crying out for* a father-figure, and shortly before this she had written *the man who protected me so often in the past will surely not abandon me now!* (S344) and so she begged Robert: *You must be everything to me, even a father – won't you, Robert?* (S387) But Robert himself was now issuing threats: 'You will write it (the letter to Schilling), otherwise I will have to break with you for a while, until you come to your senses' (S405). Clara's reaction to this resembled Robert in his worst depression: *You have made me so disheartened . . . I have been feeling quite devastated since yesterday! The words, that you could break with me for a while – I will not forget that feeling!* (S428)

The thought that after her father had withdrawn his support, now Robert, on whom she relied, might reject her, that she might have to give up his love, must have deeply upset and worried the nineteen-year-old Clara. Robert may have suspected this, because it was at moments like these that he realised his strength: 'I want to show you who is stronger. If you will not obey me, then I will embrace you so tightly that you have no breath left. That is my usual method – I really believe that the power of my love for you is great, and it will grow ever greater' (S590). His jealousy, however, was greater than his feelings of strength: in the same letter he begged Clara not to travel back from Paris via Stuttgart – which she did nevertheless on account of Henriette – and not to give a concert there.

Clara had got to know the young Henriette Reichmann in Stuttgart – she was already *a dear friend* (T7,50). In later years she would become Clara's companion on tours, but now she travelled with her to Paris as her pupil. Clara paid a visit to Emilie List on the very day they arrived, 6 February 1839, since they had not seen each other for such a long time. Pauline García was staying in the same hotel, so although she was in Paris without Wieck she was nevertheless surrounded by

Friedrich Wieck and his daughter Clara with her friends Emilie and Elise List (?). Drawing by Pauline Viardot-García, circa 1838-39.

good friends. The following day she paid a visit to Pierre Erard, who *immediately offered to send her an instrument* (T7,54). Giacomo Meyerbeer, whom she knew from her first visit to Paris, sent her tickets for the opera, so that she could hear such famous singers as Gilbert-Louis Duprez, Giulia Grisi, Luigi Lablache, Antonio Tamburini and Giovanni-Battista Rubini. Her favourite was Lablache, because *his tone is resonant and he has fire*, unlike Tamburini and Rubini: *the continual use of mezza voce is intolerable! Why does a person have a healthy, beautiful voice after all? – to let it ring out – and regrettably they do not do that* (T7,56f).

There were invitations to soirées too. She met Alexandre Dumas, Heinrich Heine and composers such as Daniel Auber,

Jacques Halévy, Friedrich Kalkbrenner, Charles Alkan, Johann Baptist Cramer and Luigi Cherubini. It was only Onslow with whom she had more personal contact – he encouraged her after her concert in the Erard salon on 16 April *to go on writing despite intrigues against her* (T7,69). Hector Berlioz had just made passing reference to her Scherzo in his review. Her debut on 21 March at a Schlesinger Matinée musicale was a success, but this was the first and last concert that she promoted herself. Nevertheless, it brought in 1000 francs. Clara had not made any real artistic breakthrough in Paris, though she was known as *the second Liszt* (S451), but what she had achieved was to survive the private and professional demands made on her, and to build up experience and connections for the future.

Wieck could read of Clara's success in Paris in the Leipzig *Allgemeine Musikalische Zeitung*, and made one last attempt to bring her back under his influence He wrote a 'heart-rending letter' to Emilie begging her, as a good friend of Clara, to approach Robert: Clara would have to 'either abandon her music and take on the numerous cares of a housewife' or amass a capital sum of her own L1,323f). Clara was writing to Robert in the same vein. After that summer she would be touring with her father *to Belgium, Holland, England, etc.*, and they would therefore *not be able to marry* next Easter (S511f). At the same time Robert sent a statement of his assets to her, that on paper guaranteed an income, but only by including the considerable capital from Clara's concerts – that Wieck would not release – and his inheritance from his brother Eduard. Satisfied by this statement, Clara begged her father for permission to marry. He then set further unacceptable conditions to which she could not agree. The break was therefore final, and Robert started legal proceedings. In August Clara had to come home from France to attend the first court hearing.

She met Robert in Altenburg *after a separation of almost a year*, and they spent *three happy days together*. Clara set out her hopes and fears in her diary on the days that followed. She *still had to withstand the next battle with her father*. Whenever she had been at home during the past three years *no day had passed when she had not had to endure hurtful insults*. She would bring nothing into her marriage since her father *even intends to withhold the earnings I made on my long tours over the last four years*. She still hoped that his *paternal love* might outweigh *his obstinacy*. And her relationship with Robert? *A woman has so much to consider, and she must remain a certain distance in the background, which is very difficult when love is so great.* However, she was aware that her *love is not just passionate*, but *now more sensible*, and she could master her *passion and hot-temper* (T7,82ff) better now than before, but she also knew that Robert was scared by the exuberance of her feelings. 'Calm down, my fiery bride', he begged, 'too much happiness achieves nothing. Marriage is different. Then there is cooking to be done etc' (S708). Another thought worried her: *will I manage to hold Robert! His intellect is so great, and in this respect I cannot satisfy him at all* (T7,82). Robert had stated his expectations of her as artist and as his wife in unmistakable terms: 'You will stimulate me, and since I shall often be hearing my compositions, you will encourage me.' But if 'you had no further appearances in public, that would be my dearest wish' (S571): an artist 'with a bonnet on her head and a bunch of keys at her waist' (S694). In his opinion 'men stand higher than women' (S525).

Clara accepted that she would *be both artist and housewife*, but *I cannot abandon my art, or I should reproach myself ever afterwards!* She wanted to contribute to their income with concerts and tours *so that Robert can live for his music as much as he wishes, and that no cares shall interfere with his lovely life as an artist* (T7,83f). She understood *why his compositions are not as well-known as they deserve to be*: they are *all orchestral in nature* and *so they are incomprehensible for the audience, since the melodies and figures are so intertwined that the ear has too much to hear and cannot disentangle all the beautiful elements.* She ranked him beside Mozart and Beethoven, and wished that he would compose for an orchestra: *The time will come when the world will recognise the third composer, but this time will come late* (T8,90f). Her *greatest concern is his health* (T7,85). In the meantime she realised that she could not save him from his darker side and nervous breakdowns. She was only twenty, but she had unusual insight for her age and could almost foresee the conflicts and problems of their future life.

When Clara arrived in Leipzig after the days in Altenburg, she found a letter from Wieck forbidding her return to the paternal home. Since Wieck believed that his daughter had been lost to a man who in his eyes might be artistically important, but was personally unstable and impecunious, he was becoming increasingly involved in unpleasant intrigues against his daughter, and was not above horrible slanders nor attempting to make it difficult for her to give concerts.

Clara only stayed in Leipzig for a few days, then went to her mother Marianne Bargiel in Berlin. She set out from there on concert tours lasting until the beginning of June 1840. In November her *Trois Romances pour le Piano*, Op 11, dedicated to Robert, were published in Vienna by Mechetti. She had composed the first Romance after the Paris tour, a melancholy piece, fast-moving with semi-quavers,

Robert Schumann the year before his marriage with Clara. Lithograph by Josef Kriehuber, 1839.

in which the theme is interwoven with the accompanying figures in evocative colours, harmonies and registers. In the third Romance, also dating from the time in Paris and originally entitled 'Idyll', the calm, rising theme at the opening is constantly changed into new musical thoughts and characters, making a piece that is diverse, although lacking unity. Clara had written the second piece earlier, with Robert in mind: *a little melancholy romance* (S585). *You must play it as you see fit, sometimes passionately, then again melancholy . . .* (S617). The framework of this piece is cleverly composed, with inventive use of melody and a crystallisation of the musical material, whose mood is of urgent longing, while the fast and passionate central section is worked into the reprise of the first. 'There is nothing to be changed in the Romance,' replied Robert, and composed his own Three Romances, Op 28. 'You complement me as a composer, as I do you. Each of your thoughts comes from my soul, as I in turn owe all my music to you' (S629). Ever since 1833 Robert had been inspired by her compositions, and had taken many of his themes from them.

In Berlin Clara found her mother in difficult circumstances; the illness, *hypochondria*, of her husband, their *unhappy marriage*, *worries about food*, all reflected for Clara the circumstances that she herself feared most (T8,94). And just at this point Robert, under pressure from the legal wranglings, was afflicted once again by anxiety attacks and depression. Clara realised that she must not show any weakness; had Robert not written recently: 'don't fall ill on me now, otherwise I will succumb too'? (S624) Then she had to contend with the contradictions in her father's behaviour – he wanted to prescribe for her how she *could best arrange her concerts* in Leipzig, yet he was doing everything in his power to prevent her public appearance in Berlin (T8,96). And as if this were not enough, Clara had to help her mother out several times with Robert's state bonds and later with her concert income. Small wonder that she remarked: *I have a great number of worries at the moment! And I am afraid for the future too!* (T8,89), and that she complained of moods that she can hardly describe: *I am discontented with myself in every way, I seem so weak at the piano . . . I feel that my spirit is so weak – it is enough to make me despair* (T8,98).

Nevertheless, she gave concerts on 23 and 31 October 1839, to *enthusiastic applause* (T8,103). There were further appearances in Stettin and Stargardt, that all brought money in. She promoted her own concerts in Berlin on 25 January and 1 February 1840, where she performed under unfavourable circumstances: she had a hand injury, and just two hours before the first soirée she felt so exhausted that she *could hardly stand upright. But everything went well*, and she gathered strength *with champagne in the interval* (T9,141), playing before the Crown Prince in a well-filled auditorium. At the second concert, where she played Robert's Sonata in G minor, Op 22, the audience was more reticent. She had been suffering from unbearable pains in her face the previous evening, and waited in vain for Robert to arrive, but once again *everything went well* (L1,392). It was this everlasting stamina and energy that Robert needed and sought in her, but which also scared him so that he shrank away.

Neither her health nor her troubles stopped Clara setting off on 5 February 1840 on a month-long tour of north Germany, accompanied by her mother. At the first concert in Hamburg she was *so fearful* that she had to play Mendelssohn's Capriccio *by sight*. But by the second concert her stage-fright had disappeared so that she could play Chopin's Concerto in F minor without problems, not least because she had received a cheering letter from Robert that restored her self-confidence. Then at her third appearance, on 13 February, the audience had *clapped and shouted* so that she had to play Liszt's arrangement of Schubert's *Erlkönig* a second time (T9,145f). For private audiences she had played Robert's *Kinderszenen* (Scenes from Childhood), his Sonata and the

Novelletten and was *over the moon* because they went down so well. At her first concert in Bremen she thought it was *dreadful for the artist* and *not at all encouraging* that the custom there was not to applaud, but at her second concert *the audience was so worked up* by Beethoven's Appassionata sonata, Schubert-Liszt's *Erlkönig* and Thalberg's *Mosesfantasie* that they *clapped and cheered* (T9,147ff). On 4 March she played the same works at her farewell soirée in Hamburg, plus the *Novelletten* by Robert, and took a profit of 490 talers away with her. She had also made life-long connections and friendships with Theodor Avé-Lallement, the organiser of musical life in Hamburg, and the Parish family.

Clara was persuaded to travel to Leipzig at Robert's insistence and after receiving a friendly letter from Liszt. She found Liszt as *dear* as ever, *full of life and wit*, and *as magnificent a performer as there ever was*. She was not convinced, however, by the manner in which he played Robert's *Carnaval* (T9,165). It was during these days in Leipzig, perhaps under the influence of Liszt, that she was troubled by the thought that she was losing *the most beautiful years of her youth*, and that after her marriage a thousand *obstacles might arise* to prevent her touring and thus earning an income, especially since Robert was of the firm opinion that she should remain at home at least for the first year (T9,170). Then she had an argument with him because he had unleashed in her *feelings of the greatest dissatisfaction* with herself and her upbringing (T9,173).

However much these two, with their distinctive characters, may have sought artistic unity in their marriage, their way of life hitherto was in neither case conducive to it. They sought closeness, but feared it too. Robert had assured her that marriage would be more difficult than he thought (S409), and married life would be rather 'prosaic', although he himself was more in need of domestic order and security than she (S361). Clara went house-hunting in July with mixed feelings – *a mixture of joy and anxiety* (T9,191). At the legal judgement in December Wieck's accusations against Robert had been thrown out, with the exception that he was an alcoholic. Clara was aware that Robert enjoyed drinking, and drank a lot; she had warned him of it often enough (S513). Robert himself admitted that he had sometimes 'not lived so uprightly' (S626). But now Wieck decided not to bring the necessary proof, and therefore there was nothing to prevent the marriage and preparations for a home. They found *a nice, cosy lodging* in the Inselstrasse (T9,192).

Clara felt very alone as an artist until shortly before the wedding, since Robert was away and she had no support from her father: *Oh God, I receive so little encouragement.* She turned this lack of confidence on herself, *I have gone backwards, as a virtuoso.* Did she need the *encouragement of an audience* to *enthuse her again?*

The house in which Clara and Robert Schumann lived in the Inselstrasse, Leipzig.

(T9,180, 186) Maybe it was for this reason that on 5 August 1840 she set off on a concert tour through the towns of Thuringia from which she only returned to Leipzig on 7 September, five days before the wedding. She played twice in Weimar for the Grand Duchess, and for the Empress of Russia, and the confidence that she gained there was just what *really animated* her (T9,199). She had an audience of a thousand in Gotha, in unbearable heat, and gave her final concert on 5 September in Weimar, to which Robert had come, to her surprise. She played the Trio from Beethoven's Sonata Op 70, No 1, Henselt's Study, *Wenn ich ein Vöglein wäre* (If I were a little bird), Schubert-Liszt's *Ave Maria* and *Erlkönig*, a Chopin mazurka and Thalberg's *Mosesfantasie. It was my last concert as Clara Wieck, and I had a heavy heart.*

The marriage took place on 12 September 1840 at ten in the morning – for Clara *the most beautiful and the most important* day of her life (T9,213ff).

Happiness and Reality

For Clara her new married life was both a joy and a shock. She and Robert kept a joint diary of their marriage for the first four years, describing not only facts and events but also their feelings and concerns – the written word as a means of communication rather than personal discussion. As soon as two weeks after the wedding there are entries reflecting the mixture of feelings that Clara had recognised beforehand. On the one hand she has *never before spent such happy days*, and is delighted by their joint study of Bach's fugues.

On the other hand she is worried by *housewifely concerns*, as such duties are quite alien to her, and feels *very out of sorts as Robert was not well*, and she is completely dependent *on his mood* and his opinion. She is jealous of his pupil Amalie Rieffel, since he considers that she plays his compositions *more exactly* than Clara herself: *I always comprehend the whole, and may perhaps overlook a small and insignificant accent*. Her playing disturbs Robert when he is composing, so she *cannot play in the morning, the best hours for serious practice*. She just has the evening hours, and then she will not even let a visit from her friend Emilie keep her from her work (Tb102ff).

This problem, one that she had not foreseen, will arise again in the future: *My piano playing gets very out of practice*, she wrote in June 1841, *which always happens when Robert is composing. There isn't one hour in the whole day for me! I just hope I don't go too far backwards* (Tb167). It was not just artistic inactivity from which she suffered when Robert was working, but also the distance he maintained, *his coldness* (Tb144).

Up until then Clara had only known the life of a musician and a virtuoso, so the time when she was not able to play the piano, having to curb her energy and dynamism, was bound to have consequences. She became *extremely melancholy*, had *neither strength nor inclination to play*, and felt *exhausted and upset* (Tb117) when she suggested a concert tour to Holland and Belgium, in October 1840, without success. Again two years later she was afflicted for days with *sad thoughts about the future* because Robert would not let her work and all ways for her *to earn some money* were cut off (Tb251). However happy she may have been in her life with Robert, she, a famous pianist and a much-performed composer, experienced moments of despair and self-doubt. In comparison with Liszt she believed that *everything is lacking in her personality to make her own way in the world* (Tb121), and Mendelssohn's impressive playing made her melancholy, when she saw Robert's *joyous look* and believed that this is something she could not give him (Tb156).

Robert had always encouraged her to compose. He was therefore very pleased to receive the three songs: *Ihr Bildnis* (Her Portrait), *Am Strand* (On the Shore), and *Volkslied* (Folksong), that she gave him for Christmas. 'She gushes here like a young girl', he remarked rather dismissively (Tb134). She therefore felt resigned when he proposed shortly after this that they should 'produce a book of songs' together to texts from the *Liebesfrühling* by Friedrich Rückert (Tb139): *I have no talent at all for composition!* (Tb141) Clara had, nevertheless, all the prerequisites for song composition: as a child she had performed her own songs in her concerts, she had listened to famous singers, and later become friends with Wilhelmine Schröder-Devrient and Pauline Viardot-García, she had learned and accompanied many Schubert songs, and had received professional training herself as a singer. It was months later, in June 1841, after she had complained again that her composition *just would not come out right*, that she *produced* four songs after a week of intensive work (Tb167). Robert chose three of these to put with his own six songs and three duets, Op 37.

Shortly after the birth of their first daughter, Marie, on 1 September 1841, these twelve songs were published by Breitkopf & Härtel as a joint opus, disconcerting the critics. They are counted as Op 12, Nos 2–4 and 11 in Clara's work.

Seldom has such happy breathless excitement been portrayed in music, with such intensity from the very first note, as in the song *Er ist gekommen in Sturm und Regen* (He has come in storm and in rain). The stirring and ebullient piano accompaniment that emphasises the words of the song does not just describe feelings, but also the moods of nature and excellently captures the double effect of the song itself. In the two more gentle songs *Liebst Du um Schönheit*

The only 'Joint Work' by Clara and Robert Schumann, 1841.

(If you love for beauty), and *Warum willst du and're fragen?* (Why do you ask others?) both piano and voice reflect the tender character of the text. Her Scherzo, Op 14, may have been written about this time as well, since Clara takes the theme and atmosphere of the song *Er ist gekommen in Sturm und Regen* and makes of it a piano piece full of fiery passion. It is this scherzo that she probably played during her tour of Russia.

It can be seen from her first concert as Clara Schumann how important it was for her to appear in public as a pianist, as well as to compose. This concert took place on 31 March 1841 in the Gewandhaus with Mendelssohn as conductor. She loved the *enthusiastic welcome* that greeted her and *gave her courage* as she *trembled with fear from head to toe*, and the prolonged *applause after each piece*, and the success of the first performance of Robert's Symphony in B flat major, Op 38, – *the symphony is so magnificient!* (W100) She had had sufficient confidence to include in the programme her song *Am Strand* (On the Shore), with its passionately moving piano part (it would be published later as a supplement in the *Neue Zeitschrift für Musik*) and also played two movements from Chopin's Piano Concerto in F minor, Songs and the *Novellette* Op 21 No 7 by Robert, as well as works by Mendelssohn and Thalberg. Concerts such as this, by 'the Schumann Couple', also pleased Robert; it was not necessary for Clara to tour, and he had the same compliments paid to him as she did (Tb157).

Their artistic companionship meant that they studied scores together too – here it was Clara who played the works. She looked for music as and where she could. There were occasional lessons, then music-making with friends like Mendelssohn, the Dutch composer Johann Verhulst, the singer Sophie Kaskel, Henselt or visiting soloists and composers such as the Norwegian violinist Ole Bull, or Moscheles. There were soirées from time to time at the Schumanns' or at Mendelssohn's house, and small social events in which she sometimes took part with misgivings, fearing that she was ill-prepared, but nevertheless they allowed her to be well-practised.

Wilhelmine Schröder-Devrient. Pastel by E B Kietz, 1838. In 1881 Clara could still remember her Fidelio, although she had died many years before: 'I don't know what I would give to hear her sing this role again! Or indeed to hear her sing anything again' (L3,414).

Clara had to wait before she could appear on the concert platform again, as Marie was born in the meantime. Clara had more joy over this birth than over any other of her eight children – *there is no greater treasure than a little angel like this* (W105). She let two months pass – later she would pay less heed to her pregnancies – before she accepted an invitation to Weimar for 21 November 1841. At this concert Robert conducted his symphony, while Clara played the Capriccio by Mendelssohn and the Fantasia by Thalberg, 'excellently' (Tb193).

At a concert given before the Grand Duchess on 25 November Clara again played a mixed programme, contrasting showy pieces with more musically challenging ones, such as songs by Robert. She also played a composition by Liszt as he had come to Weimar. When they met on this occasion, Liszt agreed to take part in their concert in Leipzig on 6 December, that would again be a joint husband and wife event: the premieres of Robert's first version of his Symphony in D minor and the Overture, Scherzo and Finale Op 52; Clara played Mendelssohn's *Capriccio* and, with Liszt, his *Hexameron* duo. Later, she remembered the great reception she herself had received, and the enthusiastic applause when she played, but immediately after the concert she was annoyed about the poor performance and reception of Robert's works. Her own playing and Robert's criticism made her unhappy as well: her *unease in Liszt's company*, the famous rival, whose playing she so admired – *it is always inspired, if sometimes tasteless* – may have unsettled her. She was sometimes concerned even then by his over-use of glib showmanship, the *chaos of dissonances* in his compositions, and the *mumbling in the lowest and highest registers* (Tb195ff).

Clara's concerts in the Gewandhaus on 1 and 10 January 1842, without Robert this time, began a busy musical year for her, at least in the early months. She was not yet forgotten, as she had feared. She was well aware how fast new names elbow out the old – she had just heard from Vienna of the highly gifted eleven-year-old, Anton Rubinstein. So she accepted the invitation for four concerts in Bremen, Oldenburg and Hamburg, where Robert's First Symphony would also be performed.

This, their first long tour together, began on 18 February. For Clara it would not end until 26 April. She stuck to her programming strategy: works by Robert, Mendelssohn, Bach, even the Sonata Op 53, by Beethoven, and at the end a showy opera fantasy by Liszt or Thalberg for the applause. This was the surest way for her to achieve success at this time, and that was what she needed. She even accepted an offer to court in which Robert was not included. Robert was unhappy in Hamburg, while Clara happily accepted an invitation to give concerts in Copenhagen – a plan she had had in mind for two years. Robert did not want to be away from his journal any longer.

This professional separation was a difficult step for Clara too, so much so that she fell ill the next day and had to cancel her concert in Kiel. But she stuck to her arrangements, even when the sea crossing was delayed for a week by storms. She arrived in Copenhagen on 20 March and immediately began to prepare for the concerts, with visits, making contacts, appearing in private circles, all in order to gain publicity for her three concerts that she was promoting herself. She was then able to earn a tidy sum with full houses on 3, 10 and 14 April. Her programmes were similar to those in Bremen and Hamburg, except that she added Beethoven's Sonata in C sharp minor, Op 27 No 2, in place of Robert's symphony, though Clara would have preferred to have worked with the orchestra herself on this if there had been sufficient rehearsal time available. She took part in three further concerts, so that she had a profit after costs of 100 Louis d'or, the *mite* that she so much wanted to *offer* Robert (Tb213).

It was with a heavy heart that she bade farewell to the city where the Danish King and his family had received her so kindly, where she had had such great success and where she had made new friends, including the composer Niels W Gade. She was

Two pages from the Schumanns' marriage journal, September/October 1840. Left page and top right, entry in Clara's handwriting, lower right entry in Robert's handwriting. These are typical of Clara's writing at the time. Her handwriting became larger and less constrained after Robert's death.

deterred from extending her tour to Stockholm by *homesickness*, and by miserable letters from Robert. In Clara's absence he had fallen back into his old ways of gambling and drinking. It would be fourteen years before she accepted Gade's invitation and visited Copenhagen again. Perhaps she had a premonition of this on her homeward journey, as she was assailed by *feelings of various kinds, that she did not wish to go into* (Tb225ff).

No sooner had she returned than domestic problems kept her busy, for Robert's illnesses always made her worry about the future. Clara would have liked to improve their household finances by further concert tours, but Robert was against this, and they could not decide on an extensive visit to America to earn some money. There were tensions and disagreements, even a *few little storms*, when Clara proposed *to put together a small capital sum* while she was still young (Tb269). Her participation in the Gewandhaus concerts, such as those on 2 October and 21 November 1842, were no great financial help, and for Clara they were not satisfying musically either, since lack of time meant that she was lacking 'that practical mechanical confidence' that is necessary for any artistic endeavour, and Robert had to admit 'for that I am responsible, and cannot change it' (Tb250).

In February 1843 Clara, heavily pregnant, went to visit her father in Dresden, where he had been living since before she was married. This was a reconciliation. At the beginning of the year Wieck had capitulated after negotiations with Major Serre about her assets and particularly about her grand piano, that Clara had found painful. Her father was well aware that Robert was now regarded as a composer of note, with many songs, chamber works and two symphonies to his credit, all written since they had married. Wieck might have feared that his dismissive attitude would find little understanding in musical circles. Clara was happy to see him again; she had suffered from the break in their relationship. The three days in Dresden were tiring all the same, because Wieck's *terrible unease, his restlessness of mind and body* meant constant excitement (Tb264). Clara's *dearest wish*, a reconciliation between Wieck and Robert, was only *effected* after the successful first performance of his choral work, *Das Paradies und die Peri* (Paradise and the Peri) on 4 December (Tb274).

Before that she had given the first performance of Robert's Piano Quintet, Op 44, in Dresden on 20 and 30 November – she had already presented it in her own matinée, and aroused *much interest* (W122). She would play this quintet many times and make it so popular that in 1845 the publishers Breitkopf & Härtel would bring out her version for piano duet, and thirteen years later a simpler version also arranged by her (H173). Meanwhile she had also attended Robert's rehearsals for the *Peri* in Leipzig – it was his debut as conductor – since 'I don't want to hold a rehearsal at which you are not present, it is as if my guardian angel is missing (L2,57).

Despite the birth of her second daughter Elise on 25 April 1843, Clara had continued working on her songs. At the end of the year her Six Songs, Op 13, to texts by Heinrich Heine, Emanuel Geibel and Friedrich Rückert, were published by Breitkopf & Härtel. They were dedicated to the Queen of Denmark, Caroline Amalie. These are deeply felt love songs, most of which were written in the summer of 1842 and during the following year. Even *Die stille Lotosblume* (The Quiet Lotus Flower) speaks of the mystery of love, and the final question 'Oh flower, white flower, do you understand this song?' is left hanging in unresolved dissonance. The longing and sadness of love unconfessed between two people in *Sie liebten sich beide* (They loved one another) stimulated in Clara

'The famous virtuoso offers, to those who like singing, a really lovely and welcome gift, a sweetly perfumed wreath of flowers . . . The poems (by Heine, Rückert and Geibel) are particularly gentle ones, the sweet odour of true poetry emanates gently from them, and the composer has set them to music with comparable delicacy'.

CRITICAL REVIEW FROM THE *ALL-GEMEINE MUSIKALISCHE ZEITUNG*, 46, 1844, NO 15, ON THE LIEDER, OP 13

some of her most beautiful and expressive melodic writing. In *Liebeszauber* (Love's Magic) she portrays ecstasy with the vibrancy and excitement of repeated chords. She presented the last two songs to Robert as a present for his thirty-second birthday in June; 'the most successful of anything she has written to date' was his comment, and Robert's *Frühlingsnacht* (Spring Night), Op 39 No 12, is itself reminiscent of Clara's *Liebeszauber* (Tb229).

Clara had been busy for a long time with preparations for the much anticipated tour to Russia to which she had persuaded, with the help of Mendelssohn, a hesitant Robert to come. Their daughters Marie and Elise were left in the care of Robert's brother Carl and his wife Therese in Schneeberg, so the tour could begin on 25 January 1844 via Berlin.

Her pleasure and satisfaction to finally be doing something

artistic again helped Clara to overcome all the unpleasantness and strains of the journey. After the second concert in Königsberg she had been packing *half the night* and had had *to get up at five in the morning and travel for the whole day*, but she still played that evening in Tilsit, even if it was just a private performance (L2,610). She nearly overslept before the final concert in Riga, the next stopping point, she was so exhausted. She gave five concerts on five days, with four different programmes, and entirely on her own, without the customary participation of other artists. She played her own Scherzo, Robert's Allegro, and works by Scarlatti, Bach, Beethoven, Mendelssohn, Weber, Chopin, Liszt and Thalberg. En route to Dorprt they were *stuck in a freezing snow storm* and only continued their journey the following day *at least 10 degrees below freezing* (Tb326). She took into account the level of education and sympathy towards the arts in Riga when constructing her programmes for the three concerts: she introduced Robert's *Des Abends* and *Traumeswirren* from his *Fantasiestücke,* Op 12, for the first time on this tour and ended her third concert, not with the customary opera fantasy, but with a polonaise by Chopin, new to her repertoire.

When they arrived in St Petersburg she went to see Pauline Viardot-García, and Henselt, who acted as her companion on the obligatory official visits, since Robert had been suffering from a cold, fever and anxiety since Dorprt, making him very miserable. He may have found the role of accompanying husband, and the circumstances that went with it, to be below his dignity, as he had on their first tour. He only found the necessary strength to conduct his Symphony in B flat major on a single occasion. At least here Clara had more time to prepare for the four concerts she was promoting herself. She had, however, to contend with the great love of St Petersburg audiences for Italian opera, and could not count on full halls. In spite of this she played Beethoven sonatas, great Romantic works such as Mendelssohn's Piano

Concerto in G minor, Weber's *Konzertstück* in F minor and Robert's Piano Quintet.

After spending nearly a month in St Petersburg, the tour continued to Moscow via Kver. On the way Robert almost passed out from the roughness of the roads. In Moscow, despite all the strains, Clara found time for three concerts, but with poor audiences, since many of the nobility had already left the city for their country estates. All the same, she could be satisfied: she had arranged and made an important four month tour without her father, reliant entirely on herself – Robert, constantly ill, was more of a hindrance than a help – and had made a profit of some 3000 talers. The 'wonderful artist', as she was known in Russia, had found acknowledgement and recognition.

The mental strains of this tour would clearly have repercussions: only three months after their return, in August 1844, Robert had a breakdown. A holiday in the Harz mountains in October brought little relief. They both decided to move to Dresden. This was not just for the climate, but primarily because the city of Berlin had invited their famous friend Mendelssohn, and it was Gade and not Robert who was appointed his successor for the coming season in Leipzig. Mendelssohn had boosted Clara's self-confidence by showing her respect and recognition at every opportunity, and he had drawn her back into the artistic world with their joint performances, both private and public. Her admiration for him was so great that Robert was angry: 'All the same – don't let us forget ourselves too much. Jews remain Jews.' Yet he himself rated Mendelssohn more highly than almost anyone else (Tb122). The sympathy between Clara and Mendelssohn was, however, stronger than the somewhat one-sided personal admiration felt by Robert. Mendelssohn had recognised in Clara a deeply convinced, and convincing, interpreter of his own works: as early as 1835 he had been pleased with his *Capriccio* for the first time when she had played it 'like a little devil', (M1,377) and she had had to repeat his *Frühlingslied* (Spring Song), three times for the Imperial family in St Petersburg. Mendelssohn had dedicated this piece to her shortly before her tour of Russia.

The Schumanns' farewell to Leipzig, on 13 December 1844, was *not made without tears*. On 5 December Clara had played Beethoven's Concerto in E flat major for the first time *after long*

The Elbe Bridge, the Hofkirche and the Hoftheater in Dresden, circa 1855. Clara found this city a provincial dead end for music: 'How much I envy Leipzig for its music' (H82).

endeavouring and wishing so. Later it would become one of her hallmark pieces: *it is the most difficult concerto I know, demanding great stamina and intellectual interpretation throughout* (L2, 77ff).

Dresden was the seat of the King of Saxony so, as Clara soon discovered, the court and the aristocracy set the tone – not an especially musical one: *Dresden is a provincial town in terms of music* (L2,95) and *a miserable existence for artists* (H52f). Nothing changed when Richard Wagner became Hofkapellmeister in 1843, nor under Ferdinand Hiller, although he did manage to inaugurate a subscription series of concerts in 1845, but he left two years later for Düsseldorf. Clara and Robert made friends with the painters Eduard Bendemann and Julius Hübner, to whose circle the sculptor Ernst Rietschel also belonged. He made the well-known plaster relief of Clara and Robert Schumann, at the request of Härtel in 1846. Robert insisted on being portrayed in the foreground, since the 'creative artist' had higher status than the 'performer'. He had remarked on an earlier occasion how he disliked it when Clara walked faster than he did when they went out, since 'a man is not happy to be 20 paces behind a woman' (Tb238).

Clara took comfort from the presence of Schröder-Devrient, who had been at the Dresden court opera since 1823. Since childhood Clara had marvelled at this singer, who had made such an impression on her as Leonore in Beethoven's opera *Fidelio* in 1822. She admired her *power and passion, her dramatic acting, and her intense phrasing* (T3,10ff). Even in old age Clara would talk of the wonderfully dramatic expressiveness of her singing.

Clara badly needed a friend like this, since Robert's moodiness and nervous condition were considerably worse. Temporary improvements, as after their holiday on Norderney in the summer of 1846, could not conceal this fact. Clara was unwilling to admit the seriousness of his illness – right up to the end the official reason was given as over-work. But she was immediately aware of what the consequences might be, and accepted his dependence on her – *what if I should die! What would my poor Robert do then!* (W150) She assumed the role of his protector and spokesman. Many of her letters to Härtel begin '*in the name of my husband*', and she insisted when making arrangements for concerts that *my husband should also take part* (H32,92).

The first performance of Robert's Symphony in C major, Op 61, had little success, because it was badly placed in too long a programme, with works by Weber and Rossini. Just eleven days later, on 16 November 1846, Clara had arranged a second performance, again conducted by Mendelssohn. Three years later, she again took trouble to put together the right programme, *because Robert's symphonies require concentration and a fresh mind* (H75). There was always the sure solidarity of their shared fates as composers – *you know how much I love him, so will understand how pleased I must be* (H71) – so she was scandalised by the cool reception for the first performance of his opera *Genoveva* in Leipzig in 1850. She never tired of arranging his works for piano: the Second Symphony, the operas, the *Scenes from Goethe's Faust*, just as she had previously arranged his choral work *Paradise and the Peri*.

'The composer demonstrates in all her work that gentle, poetic nature that marked her out, on her entry into the artistic world, as more than a virtuoso, and brought her many friends. However, at the same time the old adage that the female sex is more suited to imitation than to original creativity in the artistic realm, can also be applied to her in some measure . . . However, in Clara Schumann's writing there is many an original feature . . . The *Quatre pièces fugitives* are varied in character and style. The Larghetto, No 1 in F major, and the Andante, No 3 in D major, are the most original. There are some charming effects in the Andante, where the wide ranging figures are combined with great care. The Scherzo, No 4, simple and innocent, is reminiscent of writing for the clavier in the past, and of the smaller Beethoven sonatas'.

CRITICAL REVIEW IN THE *ALLGEMEINE MUSIKALISCHE ZEITUNG*, 47/1845, No 40, ABOUT OP 15

Clara had offered Härtel some of her own compositions, the Scherzo, Op 14, and the *Quatre pièces fugitives*, Op 15, and in early 1845 she received the proofs to correct. The four piano pieces are some of her best-known works and were published in several collected editions. They were written during her time in

Plaster relief of Clara and Robert Schumann by Ernst Rietschel, Dresden, 1846. The artist originally wanted to place Clara in the foreground, but Robert overrode him.

Leipzig. Although the dynamic is reduced – the forte passages are rare but fine and delicate – they are varied in character. In the first and third, the two lyrical pieces, there are wide sweeping melodies, rising in intensity, so typical of Clara's compositions. The agitated, scurrying staccato figures of the second piece are animated by changing harmonic colours, while the last, the Scherzo, dashes away with its sprightly theme and ends surprisingly with two forte chords.

This scherzo was originally part of the Sonata in G minor that Clara composed in the middle of January 1842. It was her first attempt at cyclical form in several movements, with which she was well acquainted from Beethoven's works, but also from Robert's. Even here, though bound by the form, she was working with contrasts in the movement of the music and dynamics, interesting harmonic progressions, and references linking all four movements in her characteristic sweeping and expressive style. She was wrong not to publish it in her lifetime – it only appeared in print in 1991 – nor did she apparently play it in public, otherwise she would not have specified the dynamics she regarded as so important just at the beginning of the fourth movement.

So, in July, from her collection of fugues, she offered Härtel those that she *had written specially for public performance* and that *she was intending to play at concerts*. These three Preludes and Fugues, Op 16, were written in 1845 after the move to Dresden, resulting from the studies in counterpoint that she and Robert had resumed at the beginning of the year (H17). They are anything but practice pieces. Clara works freely within the strict technical demands; she contrasts the shifting rhythms and hesitancy of the first prelude with a powerful and lively three-part fugue; the intimate, lyrical melody of the second prelude is followed by a fugal theme hammered out in fourths, and in the third pair she demonstrates how she can create an atmospheric prelude and a strict three-part fugue from one theme.

Between May and September 1846 Clara wrote her Trio in G minor, Op 17, for piano, violin and cello – her first chamber composition and her most extensive work so far. She was familiar with this genre, having played the Beethoven Trios, Op 70, and the D minor Trio by Mendelssohn. A gentle sadness emanates from the motif of the falling fifth, developing wistfully to the minor sixth, and this is even evident in the gently playful scherzo. Was she sad about Robert's depression that summer? Clara's Trio is, however, not at all elegiac: there are

Felix Mendelssohn Bartholdy. Edited version of a painting by Wilhelm Hensel, 1844. Clara Schumann performed 21 times with him as conductor.

far too many layers of voices woven through it, her thematic material is developed in too energetic a manner, and the many moods of the music are far too varied for that. Rather than breaking down her motifs into small fragments or relying on crass, contrasting effects, here Clara develops a flowing and lively transformation of her musical ideas. She incorporates the fugato within the structure of the fourth movement, written in sonata form as in the first movement. *There is nothing better than the pleasure of composing something oneself, then hearing it played. There are some nice sections in the Trio, and I believe that its form is also rather well executed* (L2,139), she wrote about her own work and was pleased that Härtel asked permission *to print the trio* (H39). It appeared the following year, after countless corrections. It was only when Robert had written his own chamber music for the same group of instruments, encouraged by her to do so, that she began to lose confidence, as was so often the case: *of course it remains the work of a woman,* and she calls it *feminine sentimentality* (L2,140).

It is amazing that she found the strength to compose at all, *as I cannot work as much as I would wish* (W147f). Her time was *measured out minute by minute*: she taught for *2–3 hours a day*, played *for one hour herself*, arranged *this or that for the piano*, went out walking *each day for an hour with Robert*, dealt with the correspondence, gave concerts,

Clara's children	
Marie	1841–1929
Elise	1843–1928
Julie	1845–1872
Emil	1846–1847
Ludwig	1848–1899
Ferdinand	1849–1891
Eugenie	1851–1938
Felix	1854–1879

requested all new publications from Härtel, was busy editing the German edition of Chopin's works, – her friend Pauline Viardot García was editing the French edition – coped with the household and cared for her family (W152). She gave birth to four children during the six years they lived in Dresden: her third daughter Julie was born on 11 March 1845, her son Emil on 8 February 1846 (he died in June the following year), Ludwig on 20 January 1848 and Ferdinand on 16 July 1849. At the same time she was working on her last large-scale piece: in May 1847 she wrote the first movement of a Concerto in F minor for Robert's birthday on 8 June. It remained a fragment. Robert understood why: 'Bearing children, having a husband who is always fantasising, and composing do not go together. She misses the continuity of practice' (Tb255).

She was still, however, giving concerts. During the winter of 1845-46 Clara gave the first performance of Robert's Piano Concerto in A minor, the same key as her own. She studied his work with real *pleasure*: *how richly inventive it is, how interesting from beginning to end* (L2,138). She played it first on 4 December 1845 in Dresden, conducted by Hiller, and again in Leipzig conducted by Mendelssohn, on 1 January 1846, just five weeks before Emil's birth. The following autumn, on 22 October, Clara performed Beethoven's Concerto in G major for the first time, with her own cadenza, then on 24 November she set off, with

Robert, Marie and Elise, for her second tour to Vienna, full of hopes and expectations.

'Clara was always quiet and reflective' during the journey (Tb410). Small wonder, burdened with her family, under pressure to make a success of Robert's compositions, poorly prepared and with no one at her side, as her father had been in earlier years, to cope with concert arrangements and to look after her. These were not favourable conditions for a tour. She played two of Robert's piano pieces, the *Canon* and *Romance* from Op 124, in her very first concert on 10 December 1846: five days later, at her second, she included his Piano Quintet and his *Andante and Variations*, which she played with Rubinstein. Yet she *found none of the enthusiasm from nine years previously* (L2,143). It may have been a contributory factor that the audiences were *tired of concerts* and that there was a *great shortage of money* (H45). She felt above all *like a hunted animal*. She only had *one single hour* to prepare in the evening before her third

concert on 1 January: *I am afraid that my concert tomorrow will be nothing special* (W137). Robert's Piano Concerto was not a success either; for the first time in her life she had to put a hundred guilders towards the costs.

It was only at her last concert on 10 January that she returned to her old programming strategies. She asked the celebrated singer Jenny Lind, whom she deeply admired and whom she had met in April, if she would join

Jenny Lind. Photograph by Matthew Brady, circa 1852. Clara Schumann called this singer a genius: 'What a temperament! What an artist!' (H87)

her on the platform. Clara played Beethoven's Appassionata Sonata, her success on the previous Vienna tour, alongside works by Bach, Henselt, Mendelssohn and Robert's *Traumes Wirren* (Wild Dreaming) (L2,115). It was a much applauded concert, and highly successful financially: Clara regained her self-confidence and her stage presence, even though she had, somewhat bitterly, to ascribe the success to the singer. The final matinée, where Clara performed her Trio, and Joseph Freiherr von Eichendorff was able to listen to Robert's settings of his own poems, *was one of the most interesting that we have given* (L2,151).

They returned home via Prague, where Robert's Piano Concerto was a great success, reaching Dresden on 4 February 1847, then six days later they went to Berlin for a performance of *Paradise and the Peri*. The purpose of the trip was primarily to promote Robert as composer. Clara oversaw individual rehearsals for Robert, who was despairing at the constant recasting of the singers and was ill, and she programmed his Piano Quintet as the main work at her concerts on 1 and 17 March 1847 at the Singakademie, with pieces by Bach, Chopin and Mendelssohn. Clara and Robert became friends with Mendelssohn's sister Fanny at her Sunday musical parties – Fanny was not permitted to follow a career as a musician nor to perform in public, owing to the rigid and unspoken rules applied to her elevated social position – and they considered moving to Berlin on her account. *I felt myself particularly drawn to her*

Fanny Mendelssohn-Hensel. Posthumous oil painting.

in respect of her music. Fanny's sudden death shortly afterwards, in May, *shook* Clara so deeply that their plans were abandoned (L2,161f). Fanny's brother, Felix, fell ill and died just six months later, which was an *irreplaceable loss* for both of them (L2,169): he had conducted several of Robert's orchestral works and 21 of Clara's 74 appearances as a soloist at the Gewandhaus.

During the winter of 1847-48 Clara, who was pregnant again and not feeling strong, only played in private circles, and mostly to launch Robert's Piano Trio, Op 80, – *I am passionately fond of it* (L2,173). Then from autumn 1848 she was involved in furious activity. She put on six soirées in Dresden, together with the violinist Franz Schubert, the second concert master of the Dresden court orchestra, in order to perform serious chamber music and songs with Schröder-Devrient. She was also discussing every organisational detail with Härtel for her concerts in Leipzig: the subscriptions and lists for them – a sort of advanced booking scheme in the nineteenth century – the printing and price of the tickets, the placing of announcements in the papers, as well as negotiations on the costs of renting the halls and contracts with colleagues. The performances, rehearsals and programmes were constantly changed at incredibly short notice, because musicians were ill, or other concerts clashed with theirs (H72ff). Clara could cope with the logistics of putting on a concert as competently as anyone of her time. She would continue with the soirées the following year too, since they brought in 300 subscriptions, and *a good income* as well (W155).

The period of these soirées was also a time of great political unrest. King Friedrich August II of Saxony was obliged to dissolve his old cabinet and form a liberal one, and even the King of Prussia, Friedrich Wilhelm IV, had not lived up to more liberal expectations. Clara was horrified when the uprising at the barricades of Berlin was defeated in March 1848: *over 1000 men are said to have fallen, what a thing for the King to have on his conscience*. She gave benefit concerts, with other musicians, for the Poles who had fled Prussia, and for the Saxons in the Erzgebirge, but she was disgusted at the behaviour of her Dresden friends: *these people are not at all liberal minded* (L2,178f). She admired the courage of the Saxons at the uprising in Dresden in May 1849. This took place while she was on a visit to the country and she met it with her usual decisiveness: highly pregnant, she escaped with Marie and Robert in order to protect him from attack, first to Major Serre at Maxen and later to Kreischa. Gradually she fetched all the children and their belongings from Dresden while Robert remained behind composing. The collapse of the liberal and bourgeois revolution in Germany left her wondering why the nobility still believed they were *different from us bourgeois citizens* and when *men will all have equal rights* (L2,189).

Following the Dresden soirées, Clara gave another concert in Leipzig on 14 February 1850. She performed Robert's *Introduction and Allegro Appassionato*, Op 92, for the first time, with moderate success. And then in March: back in a big city again! Whereas Robert's *Genoveva* Overture and his Piano Concerto aroused little enthusiasm in Hamburg, Clara, in her two appearances with Jenny Lind, was having great success, both artistically and financially – *incredibly full, great rejoicing* (L2,211). It was after this joint tour that Robert decided, in April, to take the position as municipal music director in Düsseldorf, offered to him by Hiller, who was moving to Cologne. Clara and Robert were in Leipzig from 18 May until 10 July, waiting for the first performance of his opera *Genoveva*. On 1 September 1850 they left Dresden, a city in which they had never felt either happy or appreciated.

The Schumanns were welcomed with much more joy, festivity and honour by the jolly Rhinelanders of Düsseldorf. The first concert conducted by Robert on 24 October was a great success. Clara appeared in her own right as soloist in Mendelssohn's Concerto in G minor – *it was the first time for many years that I had played an orchestral piece in public from memory* (L2,229). However, immediately after the concert on 6 February 1851, despite the successful first performance of Robert's Symphony in E flat major, Op 97, the first criticisms and disagreements with the orchestra and the choir began to emerge. Lack of discipline amongst the members, and also the severe illness and mental preoccupation of Robert – whose inability to conduct Clara had attempted to compensate from her position at the piano, or with hand signals and body language in the background – had all led by 1852 to disputes with the management committee. In November 1853 Robert terminated his contract.

Clara cared for and defended her husband in all disputes with the ferocity of a suckling lioness, even speaking for him as a

Clara and Robert Schumann at the pianino. Photographic reproduction from a daguerreotype by Johann Anton Völlner, Hamburg, 1850.

conductor, against her better judgement: *so wonderful, so firm, so calm* (W166). It may have been because Robert was over-sensitive to his own declining powers compared with the indomitable robustness of his wife, but at this time his criticisms both of her and her playing were particularly harsh. He was well aware that *to hear, instead of a kind word, the bitterest and most discouraging criticism* wounded Clara most deeply and destroyed her self-confidence: *what use to me is the applause of others, when I cannot please him* (L2,254f). It is possible that Clara at this time was really not at the height of her musical skills. She was thoroughly exhausted, and Robert's health and professional problems as well as a household overflowing with children were a heavy burden – on 1 December 1851 Clara's seventh child Eugenie was born. In any case, Robert effectively offloaded his own doubts and dissatisfactions onto her.

Nevertheless, Clara limited her travels to her close environs; Cologne, Barmen, Elberfeld and Bonn. The holidays that they took together were intended for him, to help his recovery: from 20 July to 5 August 1851 they visited southern Germany and Switzerland, then finally Antwerp and Brussels, where Clara made friends with her former rival Camille Pleyel, finding her to be a natural and kind person. Again in the summer of 1852 Clara and the doctor persuaded Robert, who was again suffering from severe depression, to make a trip along the Rhine and later to convalesce at the coastal spa in Scheveningen, where Clara had a *fausse couche*, a miscarriage, as she had had previously in 1846 in Norderney – a fairly common consequence of North Sea bathing in those days (W175).

1853, however, was a good and special year for Clara. In the previous September they had moved to the Bilker Strasse – their third apartment in Düsseldorf – where she not only had a room of her own, but one where she could work without disturbing Robert: *When I can study as regularly as this I feel really in my element again; it is as if a completely different mood comes over me, much lighter and freer, and everything seems much more cheerful and happy. Music is a good part of my life, after all, and if it is missing, then it is as if all physical and mental elasticity has left me* (L2,273).

She applied her renewed joy in music to composing once more. She was writing for the first time since the failure of her concerto six years previously, and between the end of May and the end of July she worked on several pieces. The Variations, Op 20,

Bilker Strasse 15, Düsseldorf. The last home shared by Clara and Robert Schumann.

are dedicated to Robert, whose *Bunte Blätter*, Op 99 No 4, provide the yearning and melancholy rheme. It is as if Clara had sought to transport the better times of the past into the present. These six variations, written *in the same form as Mendelssohn's* (H123), and *awkward to play* (L3,476), do not develop the theme itself, but rather its expression, most effectively.

The first of the *Three Romances*, Op 21, was, in fact, written last in 1855, after Robert had been taken to Endenich. This multi-layered piece, with its drawn-out dissonance, is extremely sad despite its more lively middle section. The climax in the third section seems like a cry of disillusion, while the repeated figures and semitones at the end of the piece seem devoid of hope. The second Romance, as delicately conceived as a pointillist painting, with dabbed and whispering effects in semi-quavers, fades away as if it had never really been heard at all. Clara underlined the excitement of the third

Romance with forward pushing semi-quavers and with the bass stressing the weak beats of the measure.

The *Sechs Lieder aus 'Jucunde'* (Six Songs from *Jucunde*) by Hermann Rollett, Op 23, were also written in June 1854. Clara dedicated these to her friend, the soprano Livia Frege, who had sung the Peri at the first performance of *Paradise and the Peri*. The texts for this cycle describe feelings for love and nature, and are set by Clara in a way that illustrates more than their literary content, with meditative melodies, and subtle descriptions and comments in the piano accompaniment. The various moods are well realised: the happy question and answer of the first song, measured exhilaration for the morning atmosphere of the second, the jaunty sounds of spring in the fifth song, or the rapturous euphoria conjured by nature in the sixth. Liszt arranged the third of these songs for piano duet, as he had other songs by Clara, Op 12 No 11, and Op 13, No 5.

Robert had invited Joseph Joachim to the thirty-first Music Festival of the Lower Rhine. Joachim, who was just twenty-two, played Beethoven's Violin Concerto, and this time Clara was deeply impressed. Three years earlier her opinion had been *he has neither feeling nor fire* (L2,112). Now she thought his playing *so inspired, so noble, so simple and yet touching the depths of the heart* (H105). Two months later Clara composed her *Three Romances for Violin and Piano*, Op 22, which she dedicated to Joachim. The dialogue between the instruments in the first two of these gentle and introspective romances far exceeds the writing for melody and accompaniment usually found in pieces of this kind; in the third, the lively triplets for the piano carry the violin's arching melody forward and give it a passionate character. Clara and Joachim played these romances several times at concerts.

It was on the last day of September 1853 that Clara and Robert Schumann met Johannes Brahms for the first time. He was then a twenty-year-old musician from a poor background in Hamburg and was introduced by Joachim. Brahms played his own compositions to them, and with his delicate boyish looks and high voice, his *expressive eyes* (L2,311), his long fair hair and *interesting young face*, together with personal magnetism and charm, he must have seemed extraordinarily exciting and fascinating to the Schumanns, while his music was an affirmation of everything they

Johannes Brahms. Drawing by J J B Laurent, 1853. Brahms at 20 looked as young as this when he first met Clara and Robert Schumann.

themselves had always sought (L2,281). Brahms stayed for more than a month; his influence made Robert write the essay *Neue Bahnen*, and both Schumanns agreed on a tour of Holland, from 24 November to 22 December 1853, that became the culmination of their work together. Their twelve highly acclaimed concerts contained performances of songs, and nine major orchestral and choral works by Robert. Clara played an extraordinarily wide repertoire: Robert's Piano Concerto, Piano Quintet and his Concert Allegro, Op 134, plus Beethoven's Appassionata, Waldstein and Moonlight sonatas; several works by Chopin and Mendelssohn; virtuoso pieces by Henselt and Heller; her own Variations, Op 20; the Piano Concerto in E flat major by Beethoven; Mendelssohn's Piano Concerto in G minor as well as the Konzertstück by Weber. And she played most of the accompaniments for the songs as well.

1854 began hopefully as well, with a joint concert tour in January to Hanover where they saw their new friends Brahms

Joseph Joachim and Clara Schumann. Reproduction of a missing pastel by Adolph von Menzel, 1853.

and Joachim once again. Clara was therefore quite unprepared for Robert's physical and nervous breakdown in February – she never liked to admit the seriousness of his condition. She *couldn't go to bed for sixteen days and was at his side throughout the day*. Robert and the doctors urged Clara to leave the house for fear *I might harm you when I am upset* (W179). Once before, fifteen years previously, when he felt himself persecuted by Wieck's hatred, Robert had reached a mental state that posed a danger both for himself and for Clara: 'if you had been with me yesterday, Clara, I was in a state to kill both you and myself' (S619). When Robert attempted suicide on 27 February, Clara was with her blind friend and confidante, Rosalie Leser: *I just felt something was wrong* (L2,301). It is probable that Clara suspected Robert's long-term illness to be the delayed consequence of syphilis, contracted in 1831.

On 4 March 1854 he was taken to the sanatorium of Dr Franz Richarz in Endenich. It was Robert's own wish. Clara was strictly forbidden to visit him throughout his stay there, and just a few days after he had entered the sanatorium she wrote in her anguish to the leader of the Düsseldorf orchestra, Joseph von Wasielewski: *My dearest friend, how can they do this to me, not writing me a single word about my husband! . . . It breaks my heart not to know how he lives, what he does, if he is still hearing voices, any word from him would be balm to my wounded heart! I do not look for any definitive*[47] *result, just how he is sleeping, what he does each day and if he asks for me* (R188). Robert did not ask for her. It was not until September that he asked her to write letters to him. She wrote the eighth and last of these on 5 May 1855.

Clara turned down all offers of material support except that of Paul Mendelssohn, and she soon repaid his loan. She wanted to provide for Robert and her children herself – *God has given me a talent*. She was soon teaching again: *God knows how difficult it will be for me, but I am convinced that this is the only means to keep myself going* (H116). She found comfort and support from her musician friends, Albert Dietrich, Julius Otto Grimm, Joachim, and particularly from Brahms, whom she *loves* more than *any other friend – there is a most beautiful meeting of our minds* (L2,337). He would stay nearby in Düsseldorf until Robert's death. Clara was thirty-five, and although she spoke of *motherly feelings* and of him as a *son*, agreeing that they should both use the intimate 'Du' form of address, their roles were essentially reversed (L2,354f). His *soothing, sensitive feelings* (L2,317), his *freshness of mind, his wonderfully gifted nature* (L2,337), and above all the liveliness of *his fresh and powerful personality* (L2,343), aroused in her, at least for the time being, a joy in life that she had never known before. It was he who *bore all my suffering with me, and really did all he could to encourage me* (W186). Without doubt this was no easy task as her moods swung between hope and despair, depending on the news from

Endenich. She was short-tempered and irritable, worn out with worry and work, and prone to fits of tears, lamenting her lot.

At this time Brahms was the person to whom she was closest, someone who *thinks about me, whose wishes follow mine*, someone who gives strength *when my courage threatens to disappear* (L2,352). And in him she found once more that artistic stimulation that she had been missing with Robert and new works that she could analyse intensively: *Robert's music . . . is more poetic than anyone else's, but it always feels gentle, melodious and soothing, which Johannes' music is not always, his sounds are often the opposite, they are hard . . . It is like people themselves, a rough exterior often hides the sweetest centre* (L2,385).

In June 1854 her eighth child was born, her son Felix. Afterwards she went for a summer holiday to Ostend. There she met another young man, who would be an important music partner in the future – Julius Stockhausen a twenty-year-old baritone. She firmly and successfully recommended him to Härtel, as she had other artists: *his voice is beautiful, his perception is true and deeply felt, and touches the heart* (H127).

She cultivated her contact with Härtel during this period. She offered him her Variations, Op 20, together with the Variations, Op 9, by Brahms on the same theme as Robert. They were dedicated to her and appeared that same year – a publication that would have important consequences, both artistically and personally. At the same time she advised Härtel of her Op 22 and 23, and one year later she offered her Three Romances for Piano and Violin, adding her Three Romances for Piano, Op 21, as well. With the exception of the Songs, Op 23, all these works were published in 1855. She skilfully promoted other works by Brahms too: his Piano Trio, Op 8, *this is not a trio that three people could just sight-read* but *certainly ranks alongside the most inventive and original chamber works that we have*, and his *Balladen*, Op 10, of which she had already played two for Härtel. In order to avoid any misunderstanding, she stressed, as she had with Stockhausen, that she had *no other interest* than *to promote what is beautiful*, that is, *a purely artistic interest* (H119,156).

In the middle of October 1854 she set off on a regular winter tour for the first time since her marriage. By 23 December she had given some 22 formal concerts. In Leipzig, she played for the first time Robert's Concert Allegro for Piano and Orchestra, Op 134, which was dedicated to Brahms. In Weimar she played Robert's Piano Concerto; in Hamburg it was his Quintet, his *Etudes Symphoniques* and *Des Abends* and *Traumes Wirren* from his *Fantasiestücke*, then in Berlin she and Joachim together played Robert's *Fantasiestücke,* Op 73, and the Violin Sonata in D minor, Op 121. At the same time, she put Brahms' Andante and Scherzo from his first Sonata in F minor, Op 5, on her programme in these cities.

At first I was quite worried, then I let myself be deeply glad when Brahms suddenly appeared in Rotterdam in the middle of January 1855, at the beginning of the tour of Holland. But the memory of Robert was overwhelming there, especially after she received his bleak letter from Endenich. She was worried and out of sorts, ill and weak, and in this situation even music did not help: *It is incredibly difficult to appear before the audience when my heart is breaking* (2,363f). Nevertheless she set off on an adventurous trip to Pomerania, and returned a few days later to Düsseldorf – *I needed the rest, although I cannot say that it did me any good* (H144). Then in April there were further performances of Robert's works in Hamburg and Hanover. She could only calm her inner turmoil with restless activity. She did, however, turn down the planned tour to England. She wanted to be in Düsseldorf in case *Robert should wish to see me more urgently and the doctors would suddenly ask me to come* (H142). It was Dr Richarz's letter of 19 September that finally removed *any hope of a full recovery for Robert* (L2,387).

She spent a few days walking in the Rhine valley with Brahms, and took a holiday in August with Livia Frege near Kiel, at the end of October 1855 she set off on her longest concert tour yet, lasting eight months. She gave three soirées in Berlin, again with Joachim – it was she who took care of *thousands of little concert details* – and for the first time she played Beethoven's Variations in C minor (L2,389). She returned to Düsseldorf just a week before Christmas, then in January 1856 set off for her third visit to Vienna, this time with a companion for herself and her daughters.

This was a more self-confident Clara, now considered a major interpreter of Schumann and Beethoven: she played Robert's *Etudes symphoniques* and *Carnaval, to great applause* – in Pest she even played *Carnaval* at the end of her programme. To begin she gave her audience, as she had done in Leipzig, no less a work than Beethoven's Hammerklavier Sonata. At her farewell concert she allowed herself to repeat *Carnaval* and to introduce Brahms, this time with the Andante and Scherzo from his Sonata in C major, Op 1. She tried to avoid where she could, the salon atmosphere, encouraged by Liszt: *the ladies in their huge crinolines and hair pieces, fainting from the heat* for *how badly I fit in there, with my heart full of worries and longing* and with pieces *that are not suited*. Nevertheless, she was *borne along by her audience*, and earned so much that *she could support her family for 5-6 months* (L2,397ff).

Before she returned to Düsseldorf on 16 March 1856 she took her two eldest daughters, Marie and Elise, now fifteen and thirteen respectively, to a *boarding school* in Leipzig (W188). And although Brahms tried to persuade her against the 'dangers of a tour to England', she boarded the steamer at Ostend on 8 April 1856 for a cheerless night crossing to Dover (B1,170). She returned home after three months that were overshadowed by bad reports from Endenich, and a week later, on 14 July, she went to Bonn. She left Endenich without understanding, from Dr Richarz's comment that Robert might have less than a year to live, just

The Schumann children: from left to right, Ludwig, Marie, Felix, Elise (standing at the back), Ferdinand and Eugenie. Photograph, circa 1855. Their daughter Julie is missing.

how close his death might be, and on the 23rd received a telegram that she should return immediately to Bonn. Brahms and the doctor again prevented her from visiting Robert. It was only on the 27th and the following day that she could see him: *the pain, the longing for him, just to have one more glance from him, to let him feel that I am near – I had to go* (L2,414). It was only his kind and shining, beloved eyes that she now found unchanged: *as gentle a look as ever! he . . . looked at me so lovingly, embraced me once again – this comforting memory will never leave me* (H161).

Robert Schumann died on 29 July 1856, and was buried in Bonn on 31 July: *God give me strength to live without him . . . All my happiness was taken with his death! A new life began now for me* (L2,416), a life where she alone was responsible for seven children, for whom Robert would have been a *wonderful father*

(L3,10). The eleven-year-old Julie was already living with Clara's mother in Berlin, Eugenie, aged four and Felix, aged two, were being looked after at home, while Ludwig, aged eight, and Ferdinand, aged seven, were entered in an academy in Düsseldorf. From 14 August to 23 September, she spent a holiday recovering with her two eldest sons, Brahms and his sister Elise near Lucerne.

Whatever may have been the subject of her discussions with Brahms at this time and after their return to Düsseldorf, he left on 21 October. After they had said farewell at the railway station, she returned *as if from a funeral* (L3,15). It was not the end of their friendship and love, but the end of two years spent close to one another. There was no question of Clara marrying again, after all she had been through, subordinating and limiting her life as a musician, however great may have been the admiration and intense feelings she had for the young man of twenty-three. She herself was thirty-seven.

Brahms remained unmarried. Although his letters gradually lost the undertone of passionate admiration, he would write to her years later: 'May this sincere love be of some comfort to you – I love you more than myself, or anyone or anything in the world' (B2,45).

On the day after he left, Clara again set off on a concert tour, first within Germany, and then, from 9 November to 14 December, to Copenhagen once more, at the invitation of Gade. Here she had to play Robert's Concerto and his Quintet twice – *it really took fire* (H170). Brahms returned to Düsseldorf for a visit at Christmas. During these days Clara was writing her Romance in B minor, in memory of Robert, a quiet piece full of sad yearning, with a motif reminiscent of the beginning of Brahms' Andante from his Sonata in F minor.

It was her swansong as a composer; she missed Robert's participation, and his birthdays, that had motivated her to write something of her own. She had very little peace, nor time to herself, after all the concerts that were so necessary to support her family, and she lacked a firm conviction in the ability of women to compose. Her temporary joy: *there is nothing better than producing something oneself* (L2,274), was often spoiled by the doubts she shared with contemporary society: *women can not become composers* (L2,161). Nevertheless, her works appeared in the nineteenth century in numerous new and collected editions. She would later recommend the composer Josephine Lang, who was unable to find a publisher, but she herself felt she was *called to reproduce beautiful works*, and she would achieve more as an interpreter of important new piano and chamber music works than almost anyone else (B1,599).

Concerts, Programmes, Strategies

In the nineteenth century anyone seeking to build an international career had to be a success in three cities – in Paris, Vienna and London. Offers from America, that Clara in fact declined, would follow. Wieck and Clara had tackled Paris and Vienna, but plans for England had always had to be deferred while she was married.

Clara was able to satisfy her long-cherished dream in 1856, though she had no idea that this country would become the focal point of her concert life: she visited England nineteen times in thirty-two years. She would arrive for a three-month tour in March, or in later years in January. From 1876 she shortened her stay to five or six weeks, between February and April. She gave more concerts in England than anywhere else, and most of these were in London: in 1869 there were 24 concerts in England out of a total of 33 concerts, in 1881 it was 11 out of a total 18, and between 1880 and 1888 there were 52 English concerts compared with 49 elsewhere, many of these in Frankfurt. She did not present herself in any different way than she did in Germany, remaining true to herself and her artistic demands.

Her English debut took place on 14 April 1856 with the Philharmonic Society in a typical mixed programme of orchestral works, arias, songs and solo pieces. She played Beethoven's Piano Concerto in E flat major and one of her favourite pieces, Mendelssohn's *Variations Sérieuses*. She was thus positioning herself from the outset at the musical level she would maintain in her concert programmes for the next 35 years. At that period there was some astonishment about Robert's Piano Concerto, but this did not deter her from continuing to play it, so that by the 1870s it was being performed not only by her pupils but by pianists

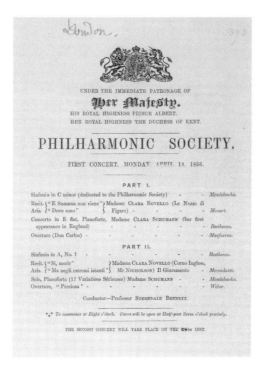

The programme for Clara Wieck-Schumann's first concert performance in England, in 1856. She courageously made her debut with Beethoven's Piano Concerto in E flat major, a so-called man's concerto.

such as Rubinstein. Things that the critics found unusual and strange during her first visit became accepted as her own personal style by the time of her next tour.

At first Clara was disconcerted by *how music is denigrated here* (K53), and that, by contrast with Vienna, *artistic stimulation is lacking, because music is really just business* (L3,201). But then she learned to appreciate *this splendid life in all its aspects*, the *wider perspective* where one could feel *less constrained* (B1,267), and the English character – *cold at first, and unapproachable . . . but once warm, then for ever* (L2,411), and she loved the beautiful landscapes and the hospitality. From 1869 her English 'home' was in Hyde Park Gate, with Arthur Burnand, a well-to-do businessman and music lover.

She was received with increasing popularity – *really just like a dear friend* (W275), and it increased as time went by- *never in my life have I had such a heartfelt reception* (L3,333). This made it easier for her to overlook artistic deficiencies. Income was *never at the same level for instrumentalists as the reception*, and in 1865 it was still *not even significant* (W248; L3,182). But 1865 marked a turning-point in Clara's English career. In Germany and in other countries her concert engagements were made through a network of personal friends and contacts, to whom she owed her appearances at subscription concerts, as a visiting artist or as promoter of her own concerts. In London, however, musical life had developed rather differently, and she could only obtain the desired engagements and fees through an agent. It was in this year that she appeared for the first time with the famous Crystal Palace Music Society and in Arthur Chappell's Popular Concerts. For over forty years Chappell had been managing these Popular Concerts at St James's Hall, which could hold an audience of 2000, with programmes containing everything except orchestral works, and Clara would make numerous appearances here. She found a mentor for newer works in George Grove, the secretary of the Crystal Palace Society, and especially for Robert's compositions. It was his wish that she should perform Robert's Concerto. Her real breakthrough with both critics and audience came with this new organisation, and with the overwhelming success she had playing Beethoven's Piano Concerto in E flat major, the piece she had chosen for her debut, although it was considered a 'man's concerto'. From then on, England became her surest and best source of income.

She must have had an unusually strong presence on the platform. Her solemn and serious appearance, her absolute dedication to the music – *art is for me is most sacred* (K54) – and her different approach to performance, all created a fascination that neither the English audiences nor the critics could resist in the 1870s and 1880s. This enabled her to play those works that she valued most highly: first and foremost Robert's compositions, which grew in popularity through her performances. At the end of the 1860s she played his *Waldszenen* (Woodland Scenes) and his *Kinderszenen* (Scenes from Childhood) in London for the first time in public, and in 1884 his Sonata in F sharp minor, Op 11, *after a day of anxiety*. She made his *Arabeske*, Op 18, so popular that *a murmur of joy went round the hall* when she played it as an encore after Beethoven's Waldstein Sonata (L3,452,476). In England she was the definitive authority on Robert's works: the sixteen-year-old Eugène d'Albert – *I believe he will become a great pianist* – went to play the *Symphonic Etudes* to her (L3,417).

She introduced Brahms in England as well, particularly his major chamber music works such as the Piano Quartet in A major, Op 26, and the Piano Quintet in F minor, Op 36, with which she had *an absolutely huge success* (L3,332). In 1873 she would have liked to introduce his Handel Variations, Op 24, to the English audience, but she had to give up playing such strenuous works because of pains in her hands and arms. In the 1870s she played a whole series of Schubert works for the first time in London: the Piano Sonata in B flat major – *I believe it was its first public performance* (L3,286), and the Sonatas in A minor, Op 42, and in G major, Op 78, as well as his Impromptus and chamber music: the Trout Quintet in A major, Op 114, the Trio in B flat major, Op 99, and the Arpeggione Sonata. She had always had Mendelssohn in her repertoire, but she performed some of his larger-scale works for the first time in London: particularly his Second Piano Concerto in D minor, Op 40, and the two Cello Sonatas. She only played shorter piano pieces by Chopin in London for the first time, such as the waltzes, the Scherzo in B flat minor, Op 31, and the Ballade in G minor, Op 23. Clara felt so sure of her audience, and so at home in England, where she was one of the most celebrated pianists of her day, that from 1865 onwards she risked staging most of her first public performances in this country.

In England, as elsewhere, it was still customary to give concerts with other artists rather than alone. Clara was soon in a position to select these herself and so she often appeared with friends such as Julius Stockhausen or with Joseph Joachim, with whom she gave 162 of her 238 joint concerts in England. When playing piano trios she included the famous Italian cellist Alfredo Piatti as well. They were so accustomed to playing together that at the end of one concert they outdid *each other in high spirits* in Haydn's Trio in G major (L3,227). It was not usual for an instrumentalist to play solo for ninety minutes. In 1867, however, Clara explicitly said that she would give a recital in Edinburgh *where I would play on my own for an hour and a half* (L3,203). Later she would give such 'Clara Schumann recitals' more frequently. This was a sort of concert that could only be given by those who were extraordinarily popular and famous.

So great was her influence in England that impecunious female teachers would make contact with her in the hope of finding a position. In 1881 she was made an honorary member of the Royal Academy of Music in London, and in 1887 she played a major part in the thousandth of the Popular Concerts, where she made Robert's Piano Quintet the focal point. After the concert there was a crowd of people waiting for her who *waved their handkerchiefs and cried 'Come back Frau Schumann!'*. She returned, aged almost seventy, the following year, 1888, for a final visit, and took her leave of England with Robert's *Carnaval* at a Popular Concert, where her audience, as always, consisted of *the elite of the musical world* (L3,487).

And so I finally returned to dear Vienna (L3,187), the city where Clara felt she was musically most at home, so that she often toyed with the thought of moving to live there. She had quite forgotten the lack of success she had had there with Robert. Her popularity was such that in 1858–59 she could double the four concerts she was promoting herself, she could perform Robert's Trio in D minor, Op 63, and by popular demand, despite her own doubts about the audience's powers of concentration, end her third soirée with pieces from his *Kreisleriana*.

This experience enabled her to develop her performance strategy the following year: she only announced three subscription concerts to begin with, then offered her audience a further series, that is a total of six concerts in six weeks. Now she might even end a programme with Robert's *Carnaval*, rather than with smaller pieces by Chopin or Mendelssohn, as she had done before. Only Brahms' Ballades in D major and B minor from his Op 10, fell *quite flat* – it was their first performance (L3,72). Clara knew how to deal with such failures: when at her second concert in 1868 she played Robert's Andante and Variations, Op 46, with Brahms himself – it was their first joint appearance in Vienna – she accepted the reserved attitude of the audience with equanimity: one mustn't *expect too much understanding for new and different* music, next year it would *without doubt be quite different* (L3,226). She had problems on her next visit to Vienna with Brahms' works too: the *really inspired and thoroughly interesting work*, his Horn Trio Op 40, *did not go down at all well* (L3,234).

Her income in Vienna was satisfactory but not overwhelming. In 1866 she had made a profit of 1000 talers, and again in 1870 her concerts were all sold out, although other performers had to fill the halls by distributing free tickets. The three concerts that she gave in 1872 with the contralto Amalie Joachim, wife of Joseph Joachim – they were *brilliant* and *the last one overcrowded* – were to be her last appearances in Vienna (L3,281). Problems with her hands and arms meant that she had to reduce her performances, and she preferred to go to England.

Although Clara had only a few formal appearances during a comfortable period of between four and ten weeks in Vienna, she also made trips to Prague and Pest, gave additional soirées, and gave lessons each day. In contrast to London, where she could repeat programmes and once even played Robert's Piano Concerto for two different societies within a short space of each other, in Vienna she was expected to play a different programme each time, and she needed to study and to rehearse the chamber music works and songs, where she herself accompanied, with her various partners. This was not all: in England she no longer had to bother with the arrangements for concerts, and her income was considerably higher.

On 7 March 1862 Clara arrived in Paris, having only decided on this visit the previous week. Madame Erard was able to persuade her at short notice to *promote her own concerts* on her own risk, since she herself would *make the material arrangements*, the sum guaranteed in an earlier offer having been too small for Clara (L3,116). The return, after 23 years, of a pianist now famous throughout the continent, was such an event that she was accorded the rare honour of playing in the Conservatoire. Clara had some misgivings about the Orchestre de la Conservatoire: *I find it technically competent, but I miss the vitality and warmth . . . it seems to me overall that they sacrifice the intentions of the composer with their striving for effects* (K71f). This orchestra was also particularly conservative: she was advised against playing Robert's Concerto, so instead played Beethoven's Piano Concerto in E flat major. Even this was too long and difficult for the critics, although the audience reaction was apparently different, since Clara reported a *storm of applause* (L3,119).

Piano works by Beethoven in the repertoire of Clara Wieck-Schumann:
Eroica Variations in E flat major, Op 35
Variations in C minor, WoO.80
Sonatas:
Op 7 in E flat major (check hand-writing, could not read very well)
Op 13 in C minor, Pathétique
Op 27 No 1 in E flat major
Op 27 No 2 in C sharp minor, Moonlight
Op 31 No 2 in D minor, Tempest
Op 28 in D major, Pastoral
Op 53 in C major, Waldstein
Op 54 in F major
Op 57 in F minor, Appassionata
Op 81a in E flat major, Les Adieux
Op 101 in A major
Op 106 in B flat major, Hammerklavier
Op 109 in E major
Op 110 in A flat major

At her own Paris concerts Clara was not deterred from each time placing an important work by Robert at the beginning, and often also at the end: the first concert began with his Piano Quintet, and the second with the Violin Sonata, Op 105 – *Carnaval* was the closing piece – and the third opened with the Piano Quartet, Op 47. She began her last soirée with the Piano Quintet, because it had been *extraordinarily popular*, and closed with the Andante and Variations, Op 46, which she played with Pauline Viardot García (K76). She introduced Brahms as well, playing his Handel Variations first to a few musicians, and then at one of her small soirées (in Paris these always began at 10 o'clock in the evening and lasted until 1 am). She had used the same strategy for Robert's unknown works at an earlier period.

She repeated her visit to Paris the following year: *it would not have been wise for me to stay away from Paris*, since one has to *return*

Programme for Clara Wieck-Schumann's concert in the Salons Erard in Paris, 1862, where she appeared with Julius Stockhausen and Pauline Viardot (this time as a pianist).

to big cities like this for several years running, then one can educate an audience for the future. But this time everything was different: *there is much that I really detest, now that I can see it clearly . . . the musicians here are no better than in London, the same sort of hacks . . . I would prefer my bread dry in Germany, with a fresh artistic mind.* On the other hand, she was very pleased with her own playing – *the Variations sérieuses were better than ever* – and Pauline Viardot used Clara's three concerts for her own farewell as a singer, performing songs by Robert. Clara was also doing pioneering work in Lyon, where she had two concerts: *up to now no one has dared risk playing a sonata by Beethoven.* But her income was not commensurate: *great glory, no money* (K155ff). Whereas her greatest success in England was still to come, this marked the end of her visits to France.

Clara set out instead the following year, 1864, on a tour of Russia lasting from February to May, taking the same route as she had done twenty years before: Königsberg, Mitau, Riga, Moscow, St Petersburg. Exhaustion, potholes, cold – not much had changed since the last tour. But now Robert's works, unknown on her previous visit, were those *with which I had my greatest success*, especially his Piano Concerto and the *Etudes Symphoniques* (L3,151). Although the *financial considerations were dreadful* (H200), Clara still risked playing in a St Petersburg theatre that seated 3000, with costs of 700 talers. The strain of this gamble may have been as heavy on her nerves as it was on her budget, but the concert paid off: 800 roubles profit after costs. Once again in Russia she did not find any *soulmates* among the other artists, but she was very grateful to Anton Rubinstein for his help, and she was touched that for the first time in her life an orchestra offered to work with her for no financial reward (L3,153f). She played about twenty concerts in all, and *found a really enthusiastic reception, and many devotees of Robert's works.* And although her earnings *did not justify the effort* (H200), she *would not have been able to achieve* this income in Germany (L3,155).

After 1856 Clara continued to visit Holland, Belgium and Switzerland – Hungary was included with visits to Vienna. The successful tour that she had made with Robert to Holland in 1853, and her own in 1855, ensured good audiences there. Clara also benefited from her long-standing friendship with the highly influential composer and conductor Johannes Verhulst. When she returned to Holland in 1860 she was welcomed with a *torchlight procession and serenade* (B1,57,297). Although three years later in Rotterdam Clara complained about all the *moving around*, that she thought was below her, and *the constant coming and going of life as a virtuoso* that she wanted to give up, she was not thinking specifically about Holland, but she was simply tired and unwell, and very disappointed that Robert's symphonies were so poorly performed (K142). Her last appearance in Holland was at a benefit concert in Utrecht in 1883, conducted by her step-brother Woldemar Bargiel, who was music director in Rotterdam from 1856 to 1874.

Clara's concerts in Belgium were arranged by Countess Baillet, whom she had met at the Music Festival of the Lower Rhine and to whom she had then played. She left Brussels, after her first visit to Belgium in 1861, with her *eyes full of tears*, as she had *not only made good friends* with the Kufferath family (L3,100), but had also achieved something *that no other instrumentalist had done before, that is to persuade the audience to really appreciate good music*, in particular works by Beethoven (Op 53, Op 31 No 2 and Op 73), Schumann (*Kreisleriana*, *Carnaval* and the Piano Quintet), Mendelssohn (Piano Trio, Op 66, Piano Concerto in D minor and the *Variations sérieuses*) and smaller pieces by Scarlatti, Bach and Chopin (W237). Later Clara only played in Brussels on her way to London.

Clara loved the Bernese Oberland, the Prättigau, the Engadine and the Rigi. There was nothing she liked better than to recuperate in the mountain air of Switzerland, and she would have liked to *inhale the Alps themselves like the perfume of their flowers*. Instead she played in Berne the year after Robert's death, on her first tour to Switzerland, and her musical impressions were *terrible*, with singing *worse than one could hear anywhere else*. She was so sorry for the *poor musicians in their rags* that, if it hadn't been for her children, she would rather have let them have all the takings (L3,30). Her next tour to Switzerland was longer, but, according to Theodor Kirchner, who had always kept in contact with Robert, and who was now living as a composer and teacher in Winterthur, it was less successful: 'She did not find favour in most of the towns, as might have been expected' (K67). Perhaps Clara's appearance did not correspond with the Swiss image of a woman. She only undertook one more short tour in 1862, with Stockhausen as conductor at her concert in Zurich, then there was a gap of fifteen years. Yet in the eighties, Basle, Utrecht and London were the only foreign cities in which Clara still appeared.

Basle, 14 November 1877.
Upper auditorium of the Municipal Casino at 19:00
Clara Wieck-Schumann with Bargheer and Rentsch (Violins), Trost (Viola), Kahnt (Cello)

Brahms: String Quartet in B flat major, Op 67 (First performance in Basle)
Schumann: Piano Quintet in E flat major, Op 44
Schubert: Second Movement from String Quartet in D minor, D.810
Schumann: Canon in B minor, Op 56 No 5
Romance in F sharp major, Op 28 No 2
Novellette Op 21 No 1

Clara gave most of her concerts in Germany in the 1860s – later they were significantly reduced owing to the extended periods she spent abroad. She was just as famous in Germany as she was elsewhere, but she never had such unreserved recognition as she did in England or in Holland. She lived in Berlin from 1857 to 1863 and again from 1873 to 1878, giving almost seventy concerts in the city, but it was only in 1877, the year before she moved permanently to Frankfurt, that she had the sort of dazzling success that she had so long desired. She gave the most concerts in Leipzig, the last in 1889, and it was here that the fiftieth anniversary of her concert career took place, on 24 October 1878, an *unforgettable day*. Her programme contained one of her own songs, Op 12 No 11, and otherwise was devoted to works by Robert. The audience received her with ovations and a shower of flowers *that completely buried me* when she came on stage for Robert's Concerto in A minor (L3,389).

Of all the large cities in Germany, it was only Munich that she *feared in a musical sense . . . since there they are fearfully backward* (W185). She hesitated for a long time, then performed in Munich for the first time in 1857, playing Beethoven's Piano Concerto in E flat major, and shorter pieces by Schumann, Chopin and Mendelssohn. She only felt at ease there when she worked with Hermann Levi as conductor (he was Hofkapellmeister in Munich from 1872 to 1896). She remained friends with him despite their differences of opinion about Wagner. Clara had played in Hamburg in her youth, but 1861 was a special year there – she not only played Brahms' Piano Concerto in D minor, but also gave the first performances of his Piano Quartet in G minor, Op 25, and his Handel Variations. She put the latter work unannounced into her programme shortly afterwards for a concert in Leipzig.

After Robert's death Clara made no concessions to her ideal of *beautiful works* (B1,599) and *good music* (W237), although she was under constant pressure to achieve financial success – she was responsible for bringing up her seven children, and later for the medical expenses of Julie, her sons and herself. She played Beethoven, Schumann, Brahms, Mendelssohn, Schubert, Bach, Handel and Chopin, doing pioneering work on their behalf in many cities. She added works to her programme, though less often, by Scarlatti, Mozart, Weber, Hiller, Ernst Rudorff, and, in England, William Sterndale Bennett, who had introduced her there. This sort of programming was adopted from the 1860s by the pianists Carl Tausig, Hans von Bülow and Anton Rubinstein, with the addition of brilliant virtuoso works by Liszt.

Clara's recipe for success lay not so much in her concessions to popular taste as in her choice of programmes and her concert strategy. For example, she reduced the high financial risk of her concert in St Petersburg by having Anton Rubinstein as conductor. However, the programme began with an unknown overture by Robert for Schiller's *Braut von Messina*, Op 100. Clara then played Beethoven's Piano Concerto in E flat major, Mendelssohn's Rondo Capriccioso, Op 14, three solo pieces by Robert in sequence fast – slow – fast (Op 32 No 3, Op 79 No 16, and Op 12 No 7) and in conclusion the brilliant *Konzertstück* in F minor, Op 282, by Weber. She had played Robert's Piano Concerto three weeks before this, not in one of the concerts she was promoting herself, but as part of a series.

Her programming method worked, since Bülow, who *had played a lot of Liszt*, was complaining at the same time about *poor audiences* in Moscow and St Petersburg (L3,155). Careful choice of timing was also part of Clara's strategy: for instance, it was only after her overwhelming success in London that she initiated a 'Schumann night', with chamber music, songs and piano works. In the same way, she attempted to find the right moment *for the first performance, when the audience is still fresh*, and before she placed a new piece in her programme she would play it to music lovers who most nearly resembled the audience, in order *to see what the effect would be beforehand* (L3,255).

There were always works by Robert in her programmes, often more than two of them. In 1881, when she played at the Gewandhaus in a concert with Arthur Nikisch – *an absolutely excellent conductor* – she herself only played Mozart and Mendelssohn, but the final work was Robert's Fourth Symphony (L3,415). Clara had a highly realistic understanding of her audience: she knew that pieces with fast changes of scene and character or with *original branching and piquant turns* or those with unexpected *combinations . . . were not comprehensible or appealing to the general audience on first hearing* and therefore were not particularly *suitable* for *concert performance* (L3,157,147). For this reason she was very cautious about playing Robert's piano works such as the *Fantasiestücke* or *Kreisleriana*, and mostly she did not play them in their entirety.

In Vienna in 1870 she played a sequence of five of the eight *Fantasiestücke*, but in her own dramatic configuration. In this way she hoped that both she herself, and the composer, would have a success. She began with the calm and flowing *Des Abends*, following this with the breathless *In der Nacht* and the humour of *Grillen*. She placed the slow and touching *Warum?* next, in order to prepare for the final piece of the work, as well as the end of the concert. She preferred to conclude with the exuberance of *Aufschwung* rather than the neat *Ende vom Lied*, since the latter gradually faded away, as was so often the case in Robert's piano cycles, and this was not likely to encourage the audience to applaud. Clara set up her finale with particular attention. She often prepared this with Robert's gentle and peaceful *Schlummerlied*, Op 124 No 16, the perfect easy listening for the audience, with its simple theme repeated seven times. This would be followed by a lively piece such as Mendelssohn's *Rondo Capriccioso*, which would then be twice as effective.

The construction of Clara's programmes followed a basic plan. She was conscious of the audience's attention span, so she placed the important large-scale works at the beginning. Often there would be a Beethoven sonata (The Appassionata, Moonlight, Tempest or Waldstein) or a piece of chamber music by Beethoven, Schumann or Mendelssohn. Then she would relax the mood with short pieces, perhaps something by Bach or Handel – she had a subscription for the collected edition of his works being published by Breitkopf & Härtel. Her programme would usually continue with works by Romantic composers, in a dramatic progression dictated by the character of the works rather than by historic considerations, as was later the rule. Her pieces had to be 'varied in character' so that they would not 'tire the audience'. Similarly, she thought about the keys of the pieces – 'no monotony, but also no harsh contrasts' – and about their length, noted with care in her repertoire book (ES259). Her programmes would often end with shorter pieces by Mendelssohn, Chopin or Schumann. As time went on she would more frequently play as her closing piece a major work by Robert, such as *Carnaval* or the *Etudes Symphoniques*, particularly suitable because of their strong climatic endings. At concerts where she was sure of her audience, these works became the rule. As early as 1856 Eduard Hanslick had noted 'absolute purity' in Clara's own programmes, in contrast to those played by others under her influence from the mid-fifties, which 'began with Beethoven' but 'ended with Kullak' (Ha105f).

Clara seldom played a complete solo piano programme. Whereas Bülow was giving a cycle of four concerts in the sixties in Leipzig, where he performed both older and more modern piano music, Clara preferred to work with artists who were her friends in the major cities. They provided her with a *good feeling of confidence* (L3,89). True, in 1844 she had given solo concerts in Mitau and Riga *which I would prefer to do always as it is best*, but this remained just a good intention (L2,62). After Robert's death she almost gave up her tour to Vienna when Joseph Joachim could not go with her. From the mid-1860s the participation of other musicians in her own

Johannes Brahms and the baritone Julius Stockhausen. In 1854 Clara successfully recommended the singer to Hermann Härtel: 'It is a long time since I have enjoyed anything as much as his singing' (H126).

concerts was reduced to perhaps a handful of songs, unless Julius Stockhausen was singing a cycle such as Robert's *Dichterliebe*. Clara would then give a solo programme lasting an hour, placed between individual groups of songs. This was customary at the time. The 'Pianoforte Recitals of Clara Schumann' from 1867 were only solo recitals if played outside London, in Edinburgh or Bath; in London itself there were always a few songs in the programme as well.

Clara seldom included her own works after Robert's death, and then mostly shorter pieces such as the Scherzi or the Three Romances, Op 22, played with Joachim, or individual songs. However, in 1873 she opened her recital in London with her Piano Trio, and in 1886 she gave the first performance in London of her Variations, Op 20 – she was then sixty-seven years old. By this time Clara had reduced her concert appearances, although she was *dreadfully bombarded with invitations* (B2,283). She withdrew gradually: she reduced the part she took in the programme, and after 1884 she no longer wished to arrange her own concerts, but would play just one or two pieces in a subscription concert.

This had less to do with her age than with her health. She began to suffer from rheumatic pain in her hands and arms in the year following Robert's death. This led to cancelled concerts and to pauses in her performing career, then at the end of 1873 to a break lasting almost two years, with just a few exceptions. Fate had dealt her some cruel blows – in 1870 her son Ludwig was committed to the mental asylum in Colditz, her mother and her daughter Julie died in 1872, and in October 1873 her father too. She had withstood these blows because *my music helped me to bear them, but now there is nothing to help me* (3,309).

Brahms' Concerto in D minor was responsible to some extent for these pains. She had played it for the first time in Hamburg in 1861. She put it back on her programme in December 1873 in Leipzig. Fifteen years previously the premiere had been a fiasco for Brahms in that city, and she now wanted to counter this as her own success was assured. Her doctors, however, diagnosed that physical and mental strain had led to over-acidity in the stomach. This was not helped by Clara's liking for cucumber salad with lots of vinegar, chestnut ice cream and pancakes with plenty of sugar. She was forbidden to eat *anything acidic, so that means everything I would like to eat* (W385).

Rheumatic pains and the piano music of Brahms took Clara, now over fifty, to her physical limits. She had to give up the idea of playing Brahms' Piano Concerto again in 1877 because of renewed pain in her arms – *and now I am to give up the idea of ever playing it again – I can only think of this with the deepest sorrow* (L3,365). In 1871 in London she had to cancel a performance of his Handel Variations as well, *because I did not have the strength* (L3,256). She learned the Paganini Variations, which she called the 'Witches variations', but she never played them in public. Her muscles could not take the strain, unaccustomed to the demands made by the stretches on her hands, while the range of the chords, leaps and passage-work in these major works were too massive and extensive for her.

Brahms understood: in 1893, with Clara's assistance, he published his 51 preparatory technical exercises for a new kind of piano writing. She used a careful selection of these for her pupils. In 1884 Clara began to suffer from problems with her hearing, and as these grew worse and her anxiety and nervousness before each concert became ever more unbearable, she took her leave of the concert platform in Frankfurt on 12 March 1891 with Brahms' Haydn Variations, to storms of applause.

However much praise Clara earned in critical reviews, she still caused great confusion among her male critics. This was not just on account of her independence and her strong and unyielding artistic personality, but also because she was a woman. This caused a multiple disordered perception of her, since musical judgement was often based on misleading concepts, or inapplicable metaphors such as 'masculine' and 'feminine'. Eduard Hanslick left no doubt as to what he understood by this: in Clara's playing there was nothing 'feminine, dissolving, oversentimental', but instead, a 'manliness in her performance' – 'everything is determined, clear, sharp as a pencil drawing'. Nevertheless Clara could not 'be called the best pianist' – the absolute measure in everything – since she lacked the strength of a Rubinstein 'in the storm of an allegro or in the long-drawn out song of an adagio'. At the same time, Hanslick was enraged at her 'tempestuous performance' of Robert's second *Novellette* from the first volume, although the semiquavers in this piece are noted in two-four time and were marked 'extremely fast and with bravura' by Robert (Ha104f,164).

A Berlin critic, on the other hand, acknowledged that the seventy-year-old Clara had played 'with notable strength of tone' (Ka83). Nevertheless Hanslick preferred the feminine 'gentle, affectionate and pensive expression' of Wilhelmine Clauss to that of Clara whose 'performance' was 'sharply accented, even in the bass' of the legato middle movement of Chopin's D flat major Impromptu A flat major'. Especially here Clara, with the 'accuracy of the beat' fulfilled exactly Chopin's ideas on melodic intensity in the forte and a stressed, cross-rhythmical bass (Ha105).

In France her *'force'* was particularly praised, as well as her *'énergie masculine'* (masculine energy) and her *'vigueur étonnante'* (surprising vigour), in short a *'sorte de virilité'* (kind of virility) that was entirely based on strength and energy, yet was *'aux dépens de la grâce féminine, dont elle est complètement dépourvue'* (at the expense of feminine grace, of which she is completely devoid). It would appear that Clara's piano playing was either 'masculine' or 'feminine', and if it was 'masculine' it must by definition be without feminine grace (Ka162f).

In England, where Clara was the first woman to play Beethoven's E flat major concerto in London in 1856, the duality of the sexes was dependent on the work – 'a man's concerto' – with corresponding consequences: 'it wanted breadth, it wanted fire, and, above all, it wanted grandeur' (Ka239).

These absurd criteria may have unconsciously hurt Clara as a composer – for here they play an important role as well. And she faced the consequences. An attitude that may have disturbed the pianist as a seventeen-year-old in Berlin (it was said 'in the coffee houses that Clara is the man and [the well-known pianist Theodor] Döhler is the woman' (F64)), she later turned into an unconditional perfectionism from which she developed her strength – *I generally pay little heed to critical reviews* (E234). After all, she had grown up in the knowledge that her father, like Leopold Mozart, saw a woman as the more suitable pianist and interpreter.

The Composer as Pianist

Clara the composer is inseparable from Clara the pianist: 'Madame Schumann, more than any other pianist, possesses the genius of the great masters' (V211). What interested Clara most as a composer was *the tone colour*, the *character*, the *melodic invention*, as well as the *melodic complexities, interesting developments, surprising and witty combinations*, the *unfolding of a richness of feeling in the smallest framework*, and this was what she reproduced with extreme care as an interpreter (L3,290; B2,527ff). It was the composer in her who paid attention to every note, every phrase, every performance marking, and sought to discover its meaning, its expression and its sense. There was a reason why each morning she studied the works of Bach, which *demanded an enormous concentration of all her mental strength* in public performance (E27; L3,287). It was Bach's polyphony that formed the technical and musical basis for her approach to every composition: to disentangle the texture of the voices, to separate the sound planes, and to present the whole score in its rich diversity. *No passage-work*, she would always comment regretfully when someone played fast notes without understanding or sense. She herself was never prepared to sacrifice a multiplicity of voices, melodies or tones in order to simplify the music for her audience. It was for this reason that Clara insisted that her students should treat the piano like an orchestra, and study each phrase and express it as if it were a separate instrument. And this was why she would not stress the melodies of the introductory theme in Robert's *Etudes symphoniques* and his Piano Concerto, but would surround them with all the rich colours of the changing harmonies (Fr222 ff).

It would have been sufficient for Clara to rely on the singing quality of her tone, the singing legato of the melody (Ka252). It is said Pauline Viardot once remarked that Clara's singing on the piano was better than her own (R293). She insisted also on a wide range of articulation: Clara was not satisfied until her daughter Eugenie 'could play every arch, every portamento, every tie exactly as it was written' in *Mai, lieber Mai* from Robert's *Album für die Jugend* (E127). Rhythms were not to be blurred either: when Clara played the sixth of Robert's *Etudes symphoniques*, the cross rhythms were so clear that it sounded as if each hand belonged to a different performer (Fr 224). This was also true for polyrhythms, such as the four quavers in the left hand against the three quarter notes in the right hand in Chopin's Study in F minor. Clara 'was able to blend a wonderful freedom of emotion within the boundaries of the strictest of rhythms!' (E239)

This unusual concision in musical performance, devoid of affectation, this clarity and straightforward presentation of the many voices and tones in even the most complicated musical processes, was sometimes seen as academic and intellectual. Clara would have nothing to do with romanticism in the misleading sense of the word, that is, with nebulous performance, with inexact rhythms, with agogic arbitrariness and tasteless sentimentality. Her performance was based on more than technique and precision, and above all came from the way she expressed *the character and the mood of the music* (W220). Clara could rely on her intuitive musical understanding – *the right feeling for a piece of music* (K122) – and on her mastery of the many piano techniques: on her leggiero – 'she was remarkably successful at expressing gentle, light and delicate writing' (Ha105) – or on her varied tonal shading, so that she could create *a great effect, even with mezzo-forte, piano and pianissimo*, – the sound could *reach the back row of the concert hall* (Fr173,221). And she achieved these gentle sounds on a *piano without a soft pedal*, where it *is much more difficult, requiring greater practice, but is incomparably more beautiful* (L3,585). Her fortissimo never sounded 'hard or ugly' (V225). She achieved this *gentleness of touch* and *density of tone* (W268) through the suppleness of her technique – *all the power and quality of sound must come from the muscles in the back* (R393). It was just this quality of sound, with its richness in overtones and its lack of hard edge, that some critics confused with a lack of strength.

It was Clara's unusual and new phrasing that controlled all her differentiation in sound and her detailed articulation. She was able to shape a phrase, of whatever length it might be, to mark it with points and accents, heavy or light, going beyond the precision of the beat, to make the music come to life and to sing. Clara marked the scores of her pupils with countless 'little slurs and dashes' (V240), indicating subdivisions in the phrasing, 'frequent little accents' to give the music additional movement and a speech-like quality (Ha105) – these can still be heard in the recording of her pupil Fanny Davies. This inner phrasing was embedded in the broad sweep of the musical lines that brought the music to life over and beyond the bar lines (Ka252). Her art of phrasing produced a performance that was later formulated by theorists: Hugo Riemann (1849–1919), who had without doubt heard Clara play when he was a student in Leipzig and when he was a teacher at the conservatory in Hamburg, wrote the *Lehrbuch der musikalischen Phrasierung* (Manual of Phrasing in Music); the Englishman Tobias Matthay (1858–1945), who was not only a pupil of Clara's friend Sterndale Bennett, but also grew up in London where Clara was a guest star, wrote *Musical Interpretation*. He sought to present various emphases of beat and phrasing by means of hidden slurs, rather as Artur Schnabel did at a later date (V240).

'Phrasing and shading', 'accents with energy but no harshness', 'gradual progression to the climax' and 'thousands of details' were the phrases used for Clara's different, personal approach to playing

Beethoven, making her the most acclaimed interpreter of his works of her day (E125). As early as 1838 Liszt had found her performance of the Appassionata Sonata 'extraordinary and strangely beautiful' (L1,201); Grillparzer even wrote a poem on the subject. Robert found the sonatas Op 27 No 1, Op 31 No 2 and Op 53 were 'quite unusually conceived, without detriment to the original' (Tb177), and Mendelssohn considered that *no one could play* the second movement of the sonata Op 101 *like I did*, Clara remembered forty years later (L3,417f).

'There was at times a greatness in her performance of this sonata [Op 13] that made the soul shake. Where others gently place bricks together, this woman conjured whole rocks and built with them a Temple of Karnak. This is how Beethoven should be played, but who can play him like this woman'. LEOPOLD ALEXANDER ZELLNER IN: *ZELLNER'S BLÄTTER FÜR THEATER, MUSIK AND BILDENDE KUNST*, 12, NO 9, VIENNA 30.1.1866, p 35.

Clara will certainly not have emphasised the heroic and martial elements of Beethoven's works; she used her personal phrasing to project the intensity and energy in the various characters and moods of his work, and despite the 'thousands of details', brought out the great sweeping phrases and the different tonal planes. There was a reason for Clara to write the beat of 8/8 into her pupil's score of the *grave*-section in the first movement of the Sonata in C minor, Op 13 the Pathétique; the dotted rhythm was to be pointed, to counteract exaggerated pathos and to heighten the drama inherent in its tense and interrogatory nature. On the other hand, nothing was further from her mind than to submerge musical expression in attention to details, which was what so worried her in Bülow: he *dissects and dismembers everything – there is no heart in it. Everything is calculated in his head* (L3,448). The sequence of tempi was also dependent on the respective character of the piece: in the Sonata Op 27 No 2, the Moonlight, the tempo of the Allegretto must be thought out in relation to the two other movements, while imperceptible changes in tempo would emphasise the character of the two themes in the first movement of Op 53, the Waldstein (E236ff).

Clara was careful to select those works by Beethoven that would form the core of her programme, alongside compositions by Robert. She played the Concerto in C minor for the first time in 1868, because *before this it had become very hackneyed*. She waited to perform the Sonata Op 110, *to me it seemed chaotic here and there*, until it had become *quite wonderfully clear* to her. She would never play a piece where she *had to admit that I have not understood it* (L3,225,22). Her attitude was such that the *wholesale performance* of five Beethoven sonatas, for instance by Rubinstein at the end of the century, seemed *inartistic* to her, since *one puts one's whole soul into that sort of a sonata, and can one do the same in five?* (B2,503). Whenever she felt she had *played indifferently* it was as if *I had done an injury both to the music and to myself* (B1,352).

Clara performed all Robert's orchestral and chamber works with piano as well as many of his songs and all his piano compositions except Op 1, 4, 76, 126, and 133 (R358f). She had worked gradually on Robert's piano music: she added the *Fantasia* and the *Davidsbündlertänze* in 1859 for it was only then that she realised how *wonderful* they are *when I play them as I feel, no longer aware of my fingers but just the mood of poetry that imbues the whole so gently and so fervently* (L3,60). She always spoke to her pupils of the essence of this music: 'rhythm and character', 'full of feeling but never sentimental'. Any over-sentimentality was always anathema to her (E126; V234).

Plaster cast of Clara Schumann's right hand, that was large, powerful, broad and with a wide stretch.

This meant over-emphasising at the end of phrases, no dragging out of the introductory theme in the Piano Concerto, and no rubato that might destroy the basic rhythm (V219). It also meant that she played the famous *Träumerei* from the *Kinderszenen* rather faster than it is usually played nowadays – the tempo in her *Critical Edition* had been M. M. crotchet = 100, but she changed this in her *Teaching Edition* to M. M. crotchet = 80. She generally preferred a brisk tempo. She was quite aware that she sometimes let the tempo *run away with her*, particularly in pieces *that I so love and play with inspiration* (R373). But the critics prove that 'too fast' for her certainly did not mean 'inexact', since *fire and passion must never be at the expense of precision*, and this was something she had been convinced of since childhood (Tb125).

Clara preferred a flowing tempo, and therefore she looked

'Frau Dr Schumann excelled herself in her performance of Robert Schumann's Piano Concerto. When the compositions (of the most outstanding modern instrumental composer) are presented with such wonderful perfection, with such a lovely and completely conceived interpretation and yet with exemplary attention to detail, then they will win the hearts of even the most resistant members in the audience. Schumann's Piano Concerto aroused the sympathies of all who heard it, thanks to the great pianist who communicated its spirit, with which she is so intimately connected, and in such an unforgettable manner. We would also point out that the piano part of this orchestral work must be considered as nothing less than a "rewarding" one. At the same time, how extremely rewarding this is also for the artist! New evidence indeed that only virtuoso technique can lead to perfection in performance, especially in "classical" music. Frau Schumann is a virtuoso in the best and most noble sense of the word.'

HANS VON BÜLOW: *AUSGEWÄHLTE SCHRIFTEN 1850–1892*, LEIPZIG, 1911, P 177

for instruments with a light action: the piano should *not be too difficult to play and should have a full and powerful sound* (W199). In her later years this was the German Steinweg. She would have liked to take it with her to London too, *instead I have to suffer*

This piano was a gift from the Grotrian-Steinweg piano manufacturer to Clara Schumann. She preferred the German Steinway because of its full sound and its light action, especially in her later years.

torments with the Broadwood (L3,425). Her choice of instrument had consequences as well, so great was her influence: on 29 August 1877 Bülow wrote to Carl Bechstein that the general movement away from his pianos, in favour of the 'wild' Harz-Steinweg, originated from Clara.

Clara did not always find playing piano concertos to be pure pleasure. The number of players in the orchestra was frequently inadequate, then there were insufficient rehearsals and often enough she was *miserably accompanied* (L3,136). She herself knew every note of the orchestral part – *I much prefer to study from the full score* – so she was doubtless not an easy partner for inexperienced conductors (L3,96). She laughed at the way conductors behaved – *the body continually twists and turns as if in permanent convulsions* – and called them *real tyrants* who knew *no mercy* (K142; L3,451).

Clara's concert career lasted for 35 years after Robert's death, and she performed thirteen works for piano and orchestra, including – *for 20 years almost the only person to do so* – the Piano Concerto in C minor (K466) by Mozart, and particularly his Concerto in D

Clara Wieck-Schumann aged 59. Pastel drawing by Franz von Lenbach, 1878

minor (K491), for which she wrote cadenzas, published in 1891. She studied his Concertos in A major (K488), and in G major (K453) where the slow movements *brought tears to her eyes*, but she never played them in public, because *the audience has no understanding of the magnificence of this music and just sits there without engaging with it, whereas we could embrace the whole world in our delight.* She knew *just what sort of music* this was: *how everything comes alive and is woven together* in the last movement of the Concerto in A major, *as if sparks were being struck from the instruments.* But she still declined to play Mozart at the jubilee concert of the Philharmonic Society in Hamburg in 1878 – *this exceptional occasion. Mozart's use of the piano is not suitable for our time, and unfortunately the public is no longer capable of appreciating his sort of concerto* (L3,97,378). Yet in 1856 she had suggested to Härtel, unsuccessfully, that she should *play an unknown concerto by Mozart (perhaps the one in G major)* (H169).

Piano writing after Beethoven had indeed come to sound so orchestral, with multiple voices and rhythms, that Mozart now sounded like filigree work, thin by comparison. Clara, however, continued to play the D minor Concerto into her old age. The last concerto she played, in 1890, was the Concerto in F minor by Chopin, as if returning once more to her youth: *my fingers can still play it, but it is too much for my nerves. This was certainly the last time!* (B2,426)

Clara Wieck-Schumann's repertoire for piano and orchestra from 1856:

Ludwig van Beethoven:	Piano Concerto No 3 in C minor, Op 37
	Piano Concerto No 4 in G minor, Op 58
	Piano Concerto No 5 in E flat major, Op 73
	Choral Fantasia, Op 80
Johannes Brahms:	Piano Concerto No 1 in D minor, Op 15
Frédéric Chopin:	Piano Concerto No 2 in F minor, Op 21
Felix Mendelssohn Bartholdy:	Piano Concerto No 1 in G minor, Op 25
	Piano Concerto No 2 in D minor, Op 40
Wolfgang Amadeus Mozart:	Piano Concerto in D minor, K.466
	Piano Concerto in C minor, K.491
Robert Schumann:	Piano Concerto in A minor, Op 54
	Introduction and Allegro Appassionato, Op 92
Carl Maria von Weber:	Konzertstück in F minor, Op 79

Feeling at home and Swansong

In October 1862 Clara bought a house – 14 Lichtenthaler Allee, in Baden-Baden. This was *after much persuasion from Elisabeth Werner and Viardot*, and because she loved the *dark and silent pine woods*. The house had a salon, five rooms downstairs, a bathroom, two kitchens, an upper floor with dormers and attics, and enough bedrooms *for all the children to be together with me in the summer* (L3,125ff).

They nicknamed the house the 'dog kennel', and moved in in May 1863. For the first time since Robert died it was possible to have some sort of family life between May and October for

Clara Schumann's house in Lichtental, Baden-Baden, 'a modest, but very nice little house' (L3,130).

the next ten years. Marie usually accompanied Clara on her 'winter campaigns', but the other six children were living as paying guests with friends, relatives or private tutors. This was not unusual, and her numerous letters to and about her children show how much Clara was involved with their lives, and how she had *thousands of concerns* for their welfare (L3,105). Nevertheless they missed their mother and being with their brothers and sisters.

Eugenie called this time together 'the happiest summers of our lives' (E22), although Clara, who was only content when she had *achieved something substantial*, still did not develop a *talent for idleness* (W268,144). They would have breakfast together in the gazebo, then the morning would be devoted to work. After Clara had practised she would go on reading the letters that she had begun at breakfast time. The next concert season had to be prepared. This correspondence took up a great deal of time; Clara would write anything up to fourteen letters a day, often several sides in length, when *her quill . . . had run away with her heart yet again* (W149). She also studied new works in Baden-Baden and revised old ones – *unfortunately my thoroughness is increasing in a troublesome manner* (B1,429). Lessons for the children were also in the morning. The afternoons continued in a more relaxed but still disciplined fashion: coffee was at four o'clock, followed by a long walk.

There were scarcely any quiet evenings at Baden-Baden. The town was too much a centre for the international aristocracy and politicians, artists, musicians and intellectuals, and too many people came to visit the Schumann house for that. *I cannot stand peace and quiet for long, I become melancholy which is terrible. The society of fellow artists* was something that had brought Clara[71] here: contact with Brahms, Stockhausen, Hermann Levi, Ivan Turgenev, Pauline Viardot, Joachim, Dietrich or Rubinstein, who all lived in Baden-Baden or came to visit (L3,125,104). And then naturally there were soirées at the Schumanns, in which friends like Pauline took part.

The young Hungarian soprano Aglaja Orgeni, a student of Viardot in Baden-Baden, found a soirée here to be the most important event of her stay. She thought Clara 'a woman of simple appearance, sound and hard-working in all respects, upright and open', but she found this group of artists to be more 'exclusive than anything one can imagine'. They were 'true aristocrats, looking down on the maggots of mankind with pride and smugness'. The whole family 'remained strangers' to her, and she even portrays the daughters as 'quite odd'. She came closest to Marie 'with her quiet and gentle, dreamy manner' (O83,88).

Aglaja Orgeni, 6 June 1863:
'Then Frau Schumann played the Trio in D minor by Mendelssohn; that was wonderful – what an artist this woman is! Her energy, her power, her mastery of all technical difficulties, but above all that spirit, the enormous breath of life that imbues all her playing!'
ERNA BRAND: AGLAJA ORGENI: DAS LEBEN EINER GROSSEN SÄNGERIN. NACH BRIEFEN, ZEITQUELLEN UND ÜBERLIEFERUNG. MUNICH, 1931.

She was Clara's oldest daughter, and reminded her of Robert, *with a character very like her father's*. She became her indispensable companion, managed the household, and remained at Clara's side until her death (L3,144). Although Clara was strict and had exact ideas of what was right for her children and what was wrong, she never fully assumed the role of mother: she herself had grown up without a mother after all. Her letters to her children were always signed just 'Clara'. In her opinion *children should be handled according to their age. They should become friends* with their parents when they were independent and could accept responsibility. She found her relationship with Marie at this time to be *the greatest happiness for a mother* (L3,240).

While Robert was alive Clara's views on the deportment of women were thoroughly conventional: women should not attend academies of art because they contained *forward young people and a lot of unseemly statues* (W132), and the good natured and genial women of the Rhineland seemed to her *at times to transgress the bounds of femininity and decency* (L2,228). When she became a widow she was quite open about her thoroughly unconventional relationship with Brahms. She also made no secret of her deep hurt when Brahms appeared curt, morose or bad tempered, or when he tried to amuse her with jokes that Clara found far from funny – her lack of humour bordered on the severe. Her claims on his attention, couched as they were in reproaches, also led to friction; she was hurt by his attraction for a time to Agathe von Siebold and again when he separated from her, as she thought of *that poor abandoned girl* – perhaps with a guilty conscience of her own (B1,297).

Clara had permitted Robert to use the intimate 'Du' form of address after their secret engagement, and she permitted Brahms its use seven months after Robert was committed to the asylum. This form of address was at the time a sign of trust and familiarity; for Clara, who in a letter to Theodor Kirchner in 1862, twice underlined the *Du*, which she did not wish to use, it was the highest measure of intimacy: *how difficult a personal relationship is afterwards*. She had had *an experience* that *for years had hurt her to the quick* (K128).

Theodor Kirchner. Photograph by J. Ganz, circa 1868. Clara Schumann was bitterly disappointed in him: 'I gave this man the best of my heart, believing that I could save him from sinking through my friendship' (L3,454).

This reference was to Brahms. She was not on intimate Du terms with Joachim or Stockhausen, nor with any of her closest musician friends who were men. This form of address was only used with female friends whom she had known since childhood: with Emilie

List and her sister Elise Pacher, with Livia Frege or Pauline Viardot. She found it difficult to use with Wilhelmine Schröder-Devrient, because for Clara *from earliest childhood she had been so revered* (L3,119). Clara's *effusive temperament*, her uncertainty as to how she should behave towards Brahms, and her exaggerated expectations, the heightened tension, disappointments and over-sensitivities that arose from this intimate friendship and trust, were all feelings that she gradually mastered: . . . *last summer {1861} I felt once more that my old and rejuvenated heart had come back to life* (K128).

Although Clara refused to use the 'Du' form of address with Kirchner, she did not wish to lose the attention of this man whom so many women admired: *You must write and tell me how much you love me* (K128). Her need for attention was almost boundless: on her first visit to England the thought that there was no one *who knows and loves me* was really *dreadful* (W189). She was *longing for Julie's loving eyes*, because she found love *as necessary for life as the air we breathe – it is for me the light in which I thrive* (L3,206). When Kirchner spent several weeks in Baden-Baden in the summer of 1863 he succeeded in getting her permission for the familiar form of address. But just a year later she withdrew the 'Du' and *this completely unusual friendship* (K193). Kirchner had reminded Clara of Robert in his appearance and in his compositions, but she was disillusioned by his inveterate gambling and the lack of character and discipline he displayed: *I wish I could eliminate this friendship from my life entirely* (L3,454).

The ten years in Baden-Baden were overshadowed by worries about her children. Elise left the family to establish herself as a piano teacher in Frankfurt. Clara had *been upset by this parting as almost never before* (L3,183). All Clara's attempts, through the good offices of Härtel, to find a place for her charming, dreamy, problem child Ludwig as an apprentice in the music business were in vain, because he was so unreliable. It was only in the summer of 1869, when he returned to Baden-Baden in a shocking condition, that she sent him to a doctor. The diagnosis was devastating – an incurable disease of the brain. He had to be committed to the asylum in Colditz in 1870. This brought back memories: *my heart is bleeding as it has not done since I went through the same thing with my poor Robert* (L3,238). Clara could not bear to see him; she apparently only visited him twice. As if this was not enough, Felix developed a serious lung cond-ition, and Julie had to be sent to spas in the south because

Julie Schumann, the third of the sisters. Brahms was fascinated by her charms.

of her weak health. In Divonne she made the acquaintance of the Italian Count Vittorio Radicati di Marmorito. Their engagement and marriage in 1869 in Baden-Baden had an effect on Brahms that Clara had not expected: *Johannes is now a changed person, he comes seldom and is monosyllabic* (L3,230). Eight years before this he had dedicated his Variations, Op 23, to Julie. He clearly admired her and saw in her a young version of Clara, who felt something similar herself: *when I am with her it is just as if I were a young girl again* (B1,573). Clara was right in her premonitions, having *warned Marmorito to be careful of Julie* (W301). Three years later Julie did not survive her third pregnancy.

The Franco-Prussian War of 1870 separated Clara from her twenty-one-year-old son Ferdinand. He came back uninjured – *who can know what effect there is on the body that will become apparent later* (W286) – and three years later married Antonie Deutsch, against his mother's advice. Clara was right once again: he had returned from the war with severe rheumatism, treated by an unscrupulous doctor with morphine, which gradually destroyed his life (W286). Clara was quite unable to share the enthusiasm of the young, and many of her friends, for this war – Brahms wrote his *Triumphlied*, Op 55, and Stockhausen wrote a patriotic song. Clara was more inclined to think *how much could be achieved in the world were it not for the vanity of man.* Even victories plunged her into *the most dreadful sadness, for they are bought with such sacrifice.* For her the war was a *torment*, a *slaughter*, a *moment of terror.* She was horrified by the *vandalism* in Paris and mourned *the many innocent and excellent people* in France (W281f,291).

This war also changed Baden-Baden: the liberal and cosmopolitan atmosphere disappeared, as did the flair of the French. Pauline Viardot sold her villa, there were no soirées and entertainments, no streams of visitors. In 1873 Clara decided to give up her house and move to Berlin. During that last summer in Baden-Baden she completed the commission from the publishers Durand & Schönewerk in Paris *to arrange 30 of Robert's songs for piano.* They were published that same year. Clara tried *to be as faithful to the original as possible, especially in tone colour.* She did not find the work easy, and might spend a whole day *thinking about one bar.* Then she left Baden-Baden in September, with a heavy heart: *I am leaving part of my life behind here . . .* (L3,291f)

This time Clara felt more at home in Berlin than she had the first time, but it was not until 1878 that she had a permanent home, where she could live the whole year round. She found *a pretty free standing house* in Frankfurt, at 32 Myliusstrasse (L3,373). She moved to Frankfurt because

Clara Wieck-Schumann's places of residence:

1819–1844:	Leipzig
1844–1850:	Dresden
1850–1857:	Düsseldorf
1857–1863:	Berlin
1863–1873:	Baden-Baden
1873–1878:	Berlin
1878–1896:	Frankfurt

she had accepted an offer from the newly founded Conservatory there.

This was not the first offer she had received of a permanent teaching position: an attempt had been made as early as 1858 to lure her to Stuttgart. In 1871 Joachim approached her on behalf of the Academy of Music in Berlin, where he had been director since 1868. She made conditions that she hoped would not be accepted. At that time her freedom of action was more important to her than the security of a permanent position: she required 4000 taler per annum for the rest of her life, five months leave and the freedom to choose her students. She also asked Joachim candidly if they *could work together without detriment to their friendship?* After all, at her age *there could be no question of subservience* (L3,268f).

Four years later, when she had to retire from the concert platform for health reasons, she resurrected the subject, and negotiated confidently with Härtel's son-in-law Richard Schöne, who was at that time deputy to the Prussian Ministry of Culture. Here again she was quite capable, as she had been previously with Härtel, of combining business with friendship. The negotiations were so protracted that the composer Joachim Raff, the director of the Frankfurt Conservatory, struck a deal with Clara in the meantime: 2000 Talers per annum, four months leave plus short concert tours, one and a half hours' tuition per day in her own house, and her daughters Marie and Eugenie who would nowadays be called her 'assistants'. It was not Raff's intention to employ female teachers, but in his view: 'I can think of Mme Schumann really as a man' (R391). Neither the musical world of Berlin nor Joachim himself could believe the news at first.

Clara had always given lessons, even on her concert tours when she stayed for a lengthy period in cities like Vienna, Paris or London. She had enjoyed this, and was pleased when she could *sow some good seeds and eliminate the weeds* (L3,50). She considered teachers in Vienna to be *at the lowest level of technical ability*

Clara Schumann's house in Frankfurt, at Myliusstrasse 32, where she spent the last eighteen years of her life.

The reception room in the house in Frankfurt, circa 1880. Clara Schumann also gave lessons here.

(B1,246), since their tuition made *no mention of interpretation*, and even less *that the music might contain character and mood* (W220). It was this aspect that she was trying to convey to her students, encouraging their imagination and expressiveness with her suggestions and insight.

To become one of Clara's students was an achievement in itself, and she was selective. *In principle she would no longer accept any student* from Stuttgart, because she could not *approve of the touch taught there.* She herself bent over the keyboard in order to produce her permanent legato by stroking the keys (Fr169), and was horrified by the cramped and rigid playing of people in Stuttgart: *they all strut about on the piano like storks* (L3,276). Her artistic demands were rigorous.

The directness of her criticism, often verging on tactlessness, was known to offend and to dishearten her students: no expression, no power, no technique, no rhythm (Fr218). Louise Adolpha Le Beau, a highly gifted composer and pianist, who studied with Clara in Baden-Baden, broke down under the continuous and perhaps unjust criticism she received. Yet Clara was greatly admired by her students, who mainly came from Germany and England.

Clara in her sixties must have seemed imposing and majestic: she was strongly and heavily built, so that she seemed taller than she actually was. In her movements and her ever-changing facial expressions she showed both calm and great liveliness. She was always dressed in black with a lace veil over her silver hair, and she immediately commanded attention. Her eyes, large and infinitely gentle in their appearance, were variously described as grey and gleaming silver, or blue. When she had played something for her students they might glow dark blue as sapphires against[76] the flush of her cheeks. Their expressiveness captivated everyone, and 'drew one in' (E118). It was notable that, when Clara was seriously ill, Brahms referred to her 'lovely eyes . . . with which for me so much is coming to an end!' (B2,617)

Clara Schumann in London. Photograph, 1887, taken during her eighteenth and penultimate tour of England.

New students were coached first by Marie or Eugenie, since for Clara musical insight was not possible without adequate technical mastery. Only then were they permitted to take lessons with Clara, that lasted for one and a half or two hours. The students were assigned to groups of three, and had to play to her twice a week. Since Clara taught in her own home they could listen to her practising in the morning before the class. According to Mathilde Verne she was 'never in a bad mood and never scolded'. She only wrote a few comments on the music itself and usually demonstrated what she meant 'by playing something over for us' (Fr217). Her method was 'suggestive rather than explanatory' (Fr162); she tried to clarify the expressive quality of the piece, and the intentions of the composer with images, always based on an exact knowledge of the score. She would accept individual ideas as long as they were plausible interpretations. Students who came to her 'with sharp eyes and ears, well prepared and with well-developed technique' benefited most from her tuition (V236). In Frankfurt her students were also invited to the private concerts and musical soirées that Clara regularly gave with Brahms, Viardot or Joachim. When Adelina de Lara had problems with what to wear for these events, Clara provided her with suitable clothes and even gave her a necklace to go with them. Clara would help her students with their careers in England too: in London she performed with Fanny Davies and Nathalie Janotha, she arranged for them to appear with Joachim, or recommended them to Arthur Chappell.

In Clara's opinion the tradition of her own playing was only continued through her daughters. Nevertheless, her students Fanny Davies, Adelina de Lara, Leonard Borwick, or Mathilde Verne, who later was to teach Solomon Cutner and Moura Lympany, maintained the Clara Wieck-Schumann tradition in England. In America it was Carl Friedberg, whose students included Malcolm Frager and Yaltah Menuhin, who brought Clara's methods to the Juillard School in New York. Despite the difference in their personalities, the recordings made in the 1930s and 1950s by Adelina de Lara, at eighty, and Fanny Davies, at seventy, demonstrate the essence of Clara's understanding of music. The timeless Schumann interpretations of these two pianists are musical mood paintings that are performed with great intensity, imagination and poetry, with unexpected phrasing and sound effects.

Although Clara gave concerts less and less often during her years in Frankfurt, she was working on new tasks. She was particularly busy with Robert's legacy. She gave permission to F. Gustav Jansen for a 'New Series' of Robert's letters that appeared in 1886, but she withheld the letters he wrote as a young man to herself. She had been editing even when Robert was still alive. She was always interested in new works, and constantly begged Härtel for printed editions and manuscripts – *I am a pest* – but he sent them gladly (H106). In October 1846 it had been works by Chopin that she wanted to see in detail. It was not just that her copies were *always rather red*, but there were places *in the manuscript that were not correct* (H40). A regular exchange developed from this: *You are giving me an early knowledge of the works, and the pleasure of a small service I can perform* (H51). The revision was completed in 1866, but Clara did not wish to be mentioned in the new Chopin edition: *I prefer not to obtrude in this way* (H204).

The *Critical Collected Edition* of Robert Schumann's works was another matter. The publishers Breitkopf & Härtel set great store by the use of her name, guaranteeing authenticity. Her *correspondence with Härtel and Brahms*, and her conscientious examination of metronome and tempo markings took up a great deal of her time from 1879 to 1887, when the project was completed (L2,400). Then in 1886 there was a *teaching edition* of his piano works, that was to contain Clara's ideas of performance, *so that at least there is a correct edition for students* (L3,442). This was quite unlike Bülow's edition of Beethoven Sonatas, and she restricted herself to metronome markings, fingerings and indications for pedalling – so necessary and instructive for both tone quality and phrasing.

Clara's pedalling in the *Teaching Edition* followed very precise musical ideas. Her indications for Robert's *Fantasia* are in themselves a lesson in the use of the pedal. They bring out the tone shading without in any way overriding the subtle changes in harmony, or obscuring dissonance. They separate the underlying tonal plane from clear melodies, they underline climaxes, bring out dissonance and suggest phrasing. Further recommendations in this edition were made by other editors such as Carl Reinecke or Wilhelm Kempff (V282f). Whereas in the *Collected Edition* Clara had almost always given the original metronome markings, here she usually recommended slower ones. This might be on account of her age, or the greater sound density and carrying quality of the new pianos, or it might be a consequence of the frequent criticism that Robert's works were played too fast.

Clara wished that the manuscripts on which she had worked *should be preserved for posterity*, so she offered them for sale to the Berlin Library. The negotiations dragged on for years (L3,498), and were finally settled in 1890: 15,000 Marks for 16 original scores. The money came at a very necessary time, when she would otherwise have had to draw on her capital. Her income was insufficient as she was giving few concerts and had taken on the guardianship of her son Ferdinand's seven children. He was suffering from morphine addiction and was incapable of supporting his family. Financial worries were nothing new for Clara. The demands of bringing up her children and financing their illnesses were greater than she was able to meet by her playing. Her friends were aware of this and donated 30,000 talers *so that I was not obliged to work myself so hard* (W307). That same year, 1873, 17,000 Talers came from Vienna as an honorary gift.

At an earlier period she had declined all financial aid, particularly that offered by Brahms, although she had taken care of his finances for years. Now, in 1888, his hopes were rewarded.

She had not refused categorically, but 'in such a friendly way' that he renewed his request to be allowed 'to lay at her feet tomorrow, most respectfully, 15,000 (with interest and compound interest!)' (L3,508).

Clara's relationship with Brahms remained lively and full of tension throughout her life. Even in old age there were sensitivities causing friction from time to time. She insisted on being the first to see his new works. He, for his part, thought that he *had bothered her with the manuscripts he had sent* if she did not react sufficiently (L3,480). Their last arguments were in 1892, over the Schumann *Collected Edition*, on which he gave her his advice. He was hurt,

Johannes Brahms in 1894, three years before his death.

calling himself a 'poor bystander' from whom Clara had turned aside 'after 40 years of loyal service (or whatever you like to call my friendship with you)'. She replied that her *personal relationship* with him had often been difficult, but that their friendship had *always survived any rubs* (L3,558ff). These misunderstandings had certainly never undermined their life-long devotion to one other.

In her last years Clara suffered from rheumatism, gout, hearing problems and headaches, all of which troubled her most in her music: *what is to happen to me if I can no longer play?*, when work was for her *always the best distraction from pain* (L3,578,537). *I am terribly sad*, she confided in despair to her diary. *Growing old is particularly hard* for an artist, because *feeling and understanding remain* (L3,573,558). Then she felt alienated from *modern virtuoso players*, causing her *real fear* (W426): *is it not just the most horrible materialism – where is the soul in these artists: where is the touch, the poetry?* (L3,522) Her sons had all died, Felix in 1879 and Ferdinand in 1891, except for Ludwig who was confined to an asylum. Eugenie, who had stayed at home with her mother and Marie, went to live in England in 1891. Elise married Louis Sommerhoff and had lived in the USA before returning to Germany to live in Frankfurt.

All was not lost: she maintained a lively interest in the new and a childlike curiosity about the unknown. She still played her piano *fairly regularly*, when circumstances permitted, and gave at least *one lesson each day* (W433). When over seventy she was delighted by Brahms' piano pieces and songs, as yet unpublished. She was able to play them through, because *except in a few places they were not difficult*. She communicated her impressions of his new works in numerous letters: *a real source of joy and admiration, of poetry, passion, deep feelings, full of the most*

Clara Schumann. Photograph by Ernst Hanfstaengl, circa 1894, two years before her death.

wonderful sound effects (L3,563). She was not going to miss a concert by Liszt's student, Sophie Menter, although she knew that this was a different school of piano-playing: *Who gives it character? Where is the reverence to perform the composition as it was conceived?* She traced this back to Liszt; *they imitate his faults, but lack his genius* (L3,438). She heard the young Richard Strauss and saw him as a gifted conductor and composer: He *surprised us with his skill and his talent*, with his *competence and his assuredness* (L3,486). Clara, a convinced anti-Wagnerian, was even prepared to visit Bayreuth, *if I could go incognito*, since *we really ought to experience everything that is epoch-making.* However, she wanted to avoid this visit being *described in all the papers by the Wagnerians as a change of heart* (W385).

Her melancholy grew during her last two years. She was mostly unable to play and had to *give up all music* (L3,599). She had already resigned her post at the Conservatory in 1892 following a severe lung infection. At seventy-five she arranged three pieces for pedal piano by Robert for two hands *as I always play them* (L3,593). They were published that same year by Novello in London. And she was persuaded by her daughters to write down some of her preludes with which she began her practice each morning.

She revived most when Brahms visited her and played his two clarinet sonatas for her with Richard Mühlfeld. Then she sat down at the piano and played Mozart's *Kegelstatt Trio* with Mühlfeld and Joachim. Clara and Brahms met for the last time in February 1895. She had twice invited guests to meet him in the evenings. He was in a *very friendly mood*, and was also especially attentive and observant, taking the other visitors aside and requesting that they tell their stories again, as he had noticed that Clara had not understood because of her deafness (L3,594). And of course he rehearsed his Piano Quintet in G minor at her house before the concert in the museum.

Her last performance was in 1896 when she played for some students. Then in March 1896 her health took a turn for the worse: she had no appetite and lost weight, becoming *as emaciated as a skeleton* (L3,607). She had a small stroke, from which she made a temporary recovery. On 7 May she wrote a loving but not completely clear birthday letter to Brahms that she did not complete; on 10 May she suffered a second, massive stroke. Eugenie returned from London in time to see Clara before she died on 20 May 1896.

Brahms had written to Joachim in April: 'The thought of losing her is no longer to be feared . . . And when she is gone from us, surely our faces will light up when we remember her?' (L3,612) Brahms was sixty-three when she died. The news of her death reached him late in Ischl. He immediately left by train, missed his connection, and had already reached Frankfurt when he learned by chance from a newspaper that the burial would be in Bonn and had been postponed to Sunday on his account. Confused, out of breath, in floods of tears, he eventually reached Bonn after a mad journey lasting forty-eight hours, just in time to join the mourners accompanying Clara's coffin to the grave. At the memorial concerts in Honnef that followed, lasting four days, he broke down in the middle of the Adagio of his Violin Sonata in G major and rushed out to the garden. He was in tears as he played the *Four Serious Songs* on the last day. He later sent these to Marie Schumann as 'a personal memorial for the death of your beloved mother' (B2,623). Brahms died on 3 April 1897, almost a year after Clara.

In her last years Clara was worried about her *adherents*, afraid *that I will be forgotten while I am still alive*. This was despite the many distinctions and honours she had received – for her seventieth birthday she was given the *Grosse Medaille für Kunst* (Grand Medal for Art) by Kaiser Wilhelm II. But the musician Clara Wieck-Schumann survived even her erroneous biographers. And the aesthetic she represented will live on. It is as applicable now as it ever was.

Index of Notes Abbreviations

The following abbreviations refer to works quoted from in the text and noted in brackets throughout:

B   Litzmann, Berthold (ed.): *Letters exchanged between Clara Schumann and Johannes Brahms,* 2 volumes, Leipzig, 1927

E   Schumann, Eugenie: *Recollections.* In: *Clara Schumann's Children,* Weisweiler, Eva (ed.), Cologne, 1995

ES   Schumann, Eugenie: *Robert Schumann. Picture of the Life of My Father,* Leipzig, 1931

F   Wieck, Friedrich: *Letters (1830-1838),* Walch-Schumann, Käthe (ed.), Cologne, 1968

Fr   Steegmann, Monica and Rieger, Eva (ed.): *Women at the Piano. The Stories of Famous Female Pianists. From Clara Schumann to Clara Haskil,* Frankfurt a.M. - Leipzig, 1996

H   Schumann, Clara: *Letters to Hermann Härtel and Richard and Helene Schöne,* Steegmann, Monica (ed.), Zürich - Mainz, 1997

Ha   Hanslick, Eduard: *From the Concert Hall. Reviews and Accounts,* Vienna, 1870

K   Hofmann, Renate: *Clara Schumann's Letters to Theodor Kirchner,* Tutzing, 1996

Ka Bodsch, Ingrid and Nauhaus, Gerd: *Clara Schumann (1819-1896),* Catalogue of an exhibition, Bonn, 1996

L   Litzmann, Berthold: *Clara Schumann. An Artist's Life - according to diaries and letters,* 3 volumes, Leipzig, 1902-1908, re-printed in Hildesheim, 1971

M   Hensel, Sebastian: *The Family Mendelssohn (1729-1847). According to Letters and Diaries,* 2 volumes, Berlin, 1880

O   Orgeni, Aglaja: *The Life of a Great Singer. According to Letters, Contemporary Sources and Recollections of Erna Brand,* Munich, 1931

R   Reich, Nancy B.: *Romanticism as Fate. A Biography,* Reinbek near Hamburg, 1991

S   Weissweiler, Eva (ed.): *Clara and Robert Schumann. Exchange of Letters,* Basel - Frankfurt a.M., volume 1, 1984; volume 2, 1987

T   Wieck, Clara: *Diaries (1824-1840),* Robert Schumann House, Zwickau, Archive No. 4877

Ta Schumann, Robert: *Diaries,* volume 2, Nauhaus, Gerd (ed.), Leipzig, 1987

V   Vries, Claudia (ed.): *The Pianist Clara Wieck-Schumann. Interpretation in the Flashpoint of Tradition and Individuality,* Mainz, 1996

W   Schumann, Clara: *The Tie of Eternal Love. Exchange of Letters between Emilie and Elise List,* Wendler, Eugen (ed.), Stuttgart - Weimar, 1996

Chronology

Year	Age	Life
1819		Clara Josephine Wieck is born 13 September in Leipzig.
1821	2	Birth of her brother Alwin on 27 August.
1823	4	Birth of her brother Gustav on 31 January.
1824	5	Marianne Wieck leave Friedrich Wieck. Clara is separated from her mother. In September she begins a systematic study of the piano with Wieck.
1826	7	Clara attends school irregularly. She is taught English and French by tutors at home.
1828	9	Wieck marries Clementine Fechner. Clara's first performance at the Gewandhaus on 10 October. First compositions.
1829	10	Clara gives piano lessons to her brother Alwin. She meets Paganini who is impressed by her playing, and with her Polonaise in E flat major.
1830	11	Visit to Dresden to appear in court circles and prepare for her debut in the first of her own concerts, on 8 November, at the Leipzig Gewandhaus. Robert Schumann studies with Wieck and lives in his house.
1831	12	Publication of Clara's Op 1. Meeting with Goethe. Tour to German cities.
1832	13	February to April in Paris. Meets Chopin. Plays his Variations Op 2 at the Gewandhaus. Clara's Op 2 published in Leipzig.
1833	14	Tuition in theory with Dorn. Her Op 3 is published, dedicated to Robert. Meets Emilie and Elise List.
1834	15	Clara jealous of Ernestine von Fricken, with whom Robert is in love. Five-month tour of Germany starting in November.

Year	History	Culture
1819	Stamford Raffles founds Singapore. US purchases Florida from Spain.	Schubert, *Trout Quintet*. John Keats, *'Ode to a Nightingale'*.
1821	Famine in Ireland. Greek war of independence begins.	Thomas De Quincey, *Confessions of an English Opium-Eater*.
1823	Monroe Doctrine: excludes European powers from interfering in politics of American republics. Mexico becomes republic. First Anglo-Burmese War.	Beethoven 9th Symphony. Schubert, Music for, *Rosamunde*, *Die schöne Müllerin* (song cycle).
1824	Charles X becomes king of France.	Byron, *Don Juan*.
1826	Seku Ahmadu conquers Timbuktu.	James Fenimore Cooper, *Last of the Mohicans*.
1828	Russia declares war on Turkey.	Schubert, C Major Symphony and Klavierstücke. Thomas Carlyle's *Essay on Goethe*.
1829	In Britain, Robert Peel founds the Metropolitan Police force.	G Rossini, *William Tell*. Delacroix, *Sardanapalus*.
1830	France invades Algeria. Revolution in Paris. Revolution in Belgium. Revolts in parts of Germany.	Hector Berlioz, *Symphonie Fantastique*. Stendhal, *Le Rouge et le Noir*.
1831	In Belgium, Leopold of Saxe-Coburg becomes king of independent state. Charles Darwin begins voyage on the Beagle.	Vincenzo Bellini, *Norma*. Victor Hugo, *Notre-Dame de Paris*. Eugène Delacroix, *La Liberté guidant le peuple*.
1832	Britain proclaims sovereignty over Falkland Islands. Turkish-Egyptian War. In Continental Europe, first railway.	Gaetano Donizetti, *L'Elisir d'Amore*. Alexander Pushkin, *Eugene Onegin*. Johann Wolfgang von Goethe, *Faust* (part II).
1833	In British Empire, slavery abolished. Michael Faraday discovers electrolysis.	Felix Mendelssohn, Fourth Symphony.
1834	South Australia Act is passed allowing for establishment of colony there. Civil war in Spain.	James Whistler dies.

1835	16	Robert ends his connection with Ernestine, and beginning of an intensive friendship with Clara. Her Op 4 is published. Mendelssohn becomes director of the Leipzig Gewandhaus concerts. First performance of her Piano Concerto Op 7 conducted by Mendelssohn.
1836	17	Robert visits Clara in Dresden. Wieck forbids further meetings. Separation of Robert and Clara lasting 18 months. Her Op 5, 6 and 7 published.
1837	18	On tour of north Germany Clara meets her mother after a separation of many years, and re-establishes contact with Robert. Wieck refuses his offer of marriage. Clara and Wieck set off for Vienna in the autumn where she has her greatest success. Her Op 8 published.
1838	19	Clara created a K K Kammervirtuosin (chamber virtuoso) in Vienna. Intensive secret correspondence with Robert. Meets the singer Pauline Viardot García. Clara's Op 9 and 10.
1839	20	Concert tour without her father to Paris lasting till August. Wieck refuses to allow their marriage, so Clara and Robert appeal to the court. Clara moves to stay with her mother in Berlin. Op 11 published.
1840	21	The court permits the marriage. 5 September last concert as Clara Wieck. 12 September marriage in Leipzig.
1841	22	Composes 3 songs for their combined Op 37. First concert as Clara Schumann on 31 March. Birth of daughter Marie on 1 September.
1842	23	Robert accompanies Clara on concert tour to north Germany, but returns home while she continues to Copenhagen. Beginning of Robert's nervous illness that recurs with ever greater frequency.
1843	24	Birth of daughter Elise on 25 April. Reconciliation between Wieck and Clara and Robert. Clara's Six Songs, Op 13.
1844	25	Joint tour of Russia from February to March. Move from Leipzig to Dresden in December.
1845	26	Birth of daughter Julie on 11 March. Publication of Op 14, 15 and 16. First performance of Robert's Piano Concerto in A minor in Dresden with Clara as soloist.
1846	27	Birth of son Emil on 8 February. Composition of Piano Trio Op 17. Robert and Clara set off for Vienna in November.
1847	28	Concert in Vienna with Jenny Lind is the only one to bring success. Death of Emil in June. Begins work on the German edition of Chopin's works. Trio published.
1848	29	Birth of son Ludwig on 20 January. Clara arranges 5 soirées in Dresden where she accompanies the singer Wilhelmine Schröder-Devrient.

1835	'September Laws' in France severely censor the press and suppress the radical movement.	Hans Andersen, *Fairy Tales*. N Gogol, *Dead Souls*. G Donizetti, *Lucy of Lammermoor*.
1836	Texas becomes independent of Mexico. In south Africa, Great Trek of Boers.	R W Emerson's *Nature* founds Transcendentalism.
1837	In Britain, William IV dies; Victoria becomes queen (until 1901). In US, Martin van Buren becomes president. In Canada, rebellions in Upper and Lower Canada (until 1838).	Charles Dickens, *Pickwick Papers*.
1838	In Britain, People's Charter initiates Chartist movement. Steamship services established between Britain and US.	In London, National Gallery opens.
1839	Beginning of Opium War between China and Britain. Britain proclaims New Zealand a colony.	Dickens, *Nicholas Nickleby*. Edgar Allan Poe, *Tales of the Grotesque and Arabesque*.
1840	In New Zealand, Treaty of Waitangi: Maori chiefs surrender sovereignty to Britain. In Canada, Act of Union joins Lower and Upper Canada.	Adolphe Sax invents the saxophone. P J Proudhon, *Qu'est-ce-que la Propriété?*
1841	Egypt declares independence from Turkey. Second Anglo-Afghan War.	In Britain, *Punch* magazine founded.
1842	France occupies Tahiti, Guinea and Gabon. Britain acquires Hong Kong.	Richard Wagner, *Rienzi*. Alfred Lord Tennyson, *Morte D'Arthur and Other Idylls*.
1843	In India, Britain annexes Sind. In south Africa, Britain proclaims Natal a colony.	Wagner, *Flying Dutchman*. John Stuart Mill, *Logic*.
1844	In Morocco, war with France.	Dumas, *The Count of Monte Cristo*.
1845	In Ireland, potato famine. In India Anglo-Sikh War.	Benjamin Disraeli, *Sybil*.
1846	Mexico-US War (until 1848). In southern Africa, second Xhosa War.	Hector Berlioz, *The Damnation of Faust*. Felix Mendelssohn, *Elijah*.
1847	In Yucután Peninsula, War of the Castes. In France, reform banquets held. In Switzerland, Sonderund War. In California, gold rush begins.	Death of Felix Mendelssohn on 4 November. Charlotte Brontë, *Jane Eyre*. Emily Brontë, *Wuthering Heights*. Giuseppe Verdi, *Macbeth*.
1848	In continental Europe, revolutions in: Sicily; Naples; Paris; Vienna; Venice; Milan; Warsaw; and Cracow.	William Thackeray, *Vanity Fair*. Engels and Marx, *The Communist Manifesto*.

1849	30	May uprising in Dresden. Clara takes Robert and the children to Maxen, then Kreischa. Birth of son Ferdinand on 16 July.
1850	31	Successful concerts in Hamburg. Moves to Düsseldorf where Robert becomes music director.
1851	32	Robert's first disputes with choir and orchestra. Birth of daughter Eugenie on 1 December.
1853	34	Beginning of close friendship with Joseph Joachim. Meets Johannes Brahms on 30 September. Robert terminates his contract as music director. Successful tour of Holland by Robert and Clara. Composition of Op 20, 21, 22 and 23.
1854	35	Attempted suicide by Robert on 27 February. He enters the asylum in Endenich on 4 March. Brahms moves to Düsseldorf. Birth of son Felix on 11 June. Clara resumes her concert career. Meets the baritone Julius Stockhausen.
1855	36	Tour of Holland and Pomerania. Holiday with Brahms in the Rhineland.
1856	37	Concert tour to Vienna, and first tour to England. Visits Robert on 24 July. He dies two days later. Writes her last composition, the Romanze in B minor. Brahms returns to Hamburg in October. Clara sets off for concerts in Denmark.
1857	38	Second tour to England. Moves to Berlin in the autumn. Pains in her arms prevent her playing concerts at the end of the year.
1861	42	First performance of Brahms' Piano Quartet in G minor, Op 25 and his Handel Variations in Hamburg. Plays his Piano Concerto in D minor for first time.
1862	43	Concert tour to Paris after absence of 13 years. Buys a house in Lichtental near Baden-Baden in autumn.
1863	44	Moves to Baden-Baden, where for the next 10 years she spends the summers with her children. Last visit to Paris, where she appears with Pauline Viardot at her farewell concerts.
1864	45	Successful tour of Russia.
1865	46	Breakthrough with audiences and critics in England.
1867	48	Finishes editing Chopin's works.
1869	50	Julie marries Count Vittorio Radicati di Marmorito.
1870	51	Ludwig enters the mental asylum in Colditz. Ferdinand fights in the Franco-Prussian War.

1849	In Rome, republic proclaimed; French troops take Rome.	Dickens, *David Copperfield*.
1850	J W Brett lays first submarine cable, between Dover and Calais.	Nathanial Hawthorne, *The Scarlet Letter*. Honoré de Balzac dies.
1851	In France, Louis Napoleon leads coup d'état. Isaac Singer invents sewing machine.	Herman Melville, *Moby Dick*.
1853	France annexes New Caledonia. Russia conquers Kazakhstan.	Verdi, *Il Trovatore* and *La Traviata*.
1854	In US, Republican Party founded. Pope Pius X declare the dogma of Immaculate Conception of Blessed Virgin Mary to be an article of faith.	Hector Berlioz, *L'enfance du Christ*. *Le Figaro*, Paris, issued.
1855	In Russia, Nicholas I dies; Alexander II becomes tsar. In southern Africa, David Livingstone 'discovers' Victoria Falls.	Robert Browning, *Men and Women*. Gaskell, *North and South*. Walt Whitman, *Leaves of Grass*.
1856	Treaty of Paris: integrity of Turkey is recognized. Second Anglo-Chinese war. Henry Bessemer discovers process of converting iron into steel.	Liszt, *Hungarian Rhapsodies*. Gustave Flaubert, *Madame Bovary*.
1857	In India, mutiny against the British. Laying the cable under Atlantic Ocean begins.	Jaques Offenbach, *Orpheus in the Underworld*. Anthony Trollope, *Barchester Towers*.
1861	In Britain, death of Prince Albert. In Prussia, death of Frederick William IV of Prussia. In US, Abraham Lincoln becomes president.	Dickens, Great Expectations. Eliot, Silas Marner.
1862	In Prussia, Otto von Bismarck becomes premier.	Verdi, *La Forza del Destino*. Turgenev, *Fathers and Sons*.
1863	In US, slavery abolished. Polish uprising against Russia. In Asia, Cambodia becomes French protectorate.	Berlioz, *The Trojans* (part I). Charles Kingsley, *The Water Babies*. Manet, *Déjeuner sur l'herbe*.
1864	Henri Dunant founds Red Cross.	Anton Bruckner, Mass No 1 in D minor.
1865	End of transport of convicts to Australia.	Lewis Carroll, *Alice's Adventures in Wonderland*.
1867	Prussia forms North German Confederation.	Joseph Strauss, *The Blue Danube*.
1869	Suez Canal opens.	Wagner, *The Rhinegold*.
1870	Franco-Prussian War.	Clément Delibes, *Coppélia*.

1872	53	Death of Clara's mother, and of her daughter Julie from TB.
1873	54	Death of Clara's father. Sells the house in Baden-Baden and moves with Marie and Eugenie to Berlin. Arranges 30 of Robert's songs for the piano.
1874	55	Following a performance of Brahms' Piano Concerto in D minor, rheumatism forces her to give up concert performance for two years.
1875	56	Negotiations with Berlin Music Academy.
1878	59	Final negotiations with Hoch Conservatory for teaching position. Moves to Frankfurt. Celebrates golden jubilee of concert performance in Leipzig. Receives Gold Medal from King of Bavaria.
1879	60	Death of Felix from TB. Restricts her concert performances. Working on the Critical Edition on Robert's works until 1886.
1881	62	Honorary membership of the Royal Academy of Music
1886	67	Publication of her edition of Robert's early letters. Work on the teaching edition of Robert's piano works.
1889	70	On her 70th birthday receives the Grand Medal for Art from Kaiser Wilhelm II.
1890	71	Sells 16 of Robert's autograph scores for 15,000 marks to the Berlin library.
1891	72	Gives her last concert on 12 March. Death of Ferdinand.
1892	73	Retires from teaching due to ill health.
1895	76	Last visit by Brahms in February. Arranges Robert's 3 sketches for Pedal Piano, Op 56 and 58, for piano. Writes down her own preludes.
1896	76	Death on 20 May following second stroke.

1872	In Philippines, rebellion against Spain.	Thomas Hardy, *Under the Greenwood Tree.*
1873	In Spain, Amadeo I abdicates; republic proclaimed. In Africa, Ashanti War begins. In Asia, Acheh War. Great Depression.	Arthur Rimbaud, *A Season in Hell.* Walter Pater, *Studies in the History of the Renaissance.* Claude Monet: *Impression: soleil levant.*
1874	In Britain, Benjamin Disraeli becomes prime minister. In Spain, Alfonso XII establishes constitutional monarchy.	J Strauss, *Die Fledermaus.* In Paris, first Impressionist exhibition.
1878	Congress of Berlin resolves Balkan crisis. Serbia becomes independent. Britain gains Cyprus. In London electric street lighting.	Tchaikovsky, *Swan Lake.*
1879	Germany and Austria-Hungary form Dual Alliance. In Africa, Zulu War.	Ibsen, *The Doll's House.* August Strindberg, *The Red Room.*
1881	In Russia, Alexander II assassinated. In Japan, political parties established.	Offenbach, *The Tales of Hoffmann.* Henry James, *Portrait of a Lady.*
1886	In Cuba slavery abolished. In India, first meeting of National Congress. In Canada, Canadian Pacific Railway completed.	Stevenson, *Dr Jekyll and Mr Hyde.* Rimbaud, *Les Illuminations.* Leo Tolstoy, *The Death of Ivan Ilich.*
1889	Second Socialist International. Italy invades Somalia and Ethiopia. In Paris, Eiffel Tower completed. Brazil proclaims itself a republic.	Richard Strauss, *Don Juan.* Verdi, *Falstaff.* George Bernard Shaw, *Fabian Essays.*
1890	In Germany, Otto von Bismarck dismissed. In Spain, universal suffrage.	Tchaikovsky, *The Queen of Spades.* Ibsen, *Hedda Gabler.*
1891	Building of Trans-Siberian railway begins. Shearers' strike in Australia.	Tchaikovsky, *The Nutcracker.* Oscar Wilde, *The Picture of Dorian Gray.* Toulouse-Lautrec, *Le bal du Moulin-Rouge.*
1892	The Panama scandal breaks in France. Charles Cross discovers viscose. Rudolf Diesel patents a new type of internal combustion engine.	Alfred Tennyson dies. Walt Whitman dies.
1895	In Britain, Lord Salisbury becomes prime minister. Cuban rebellion begins. Japan conquers Taiwan (Formosa). Wilhelm Röntgen invents X-rays.	H G Wells, *The Time Machine.* W B Yeats, *Poems.* Marconi sends message over a mile by wireless. Sigmund Freud publishes first work on psychoanalysis.
1896	Theodore Herzl founds Zionism. First Olympic Games of the modern era held in Athens. Antoine Becquerel discovers radioactivity of uranium.	Puccini, *La Bohème.* Thomas Hardy, *Jude the Obscure.* Nobel Prizes established.

Clara Schumann List of Works

Songs:

Alte heimat (Kerner) (1831 lost)

Der Traum von Tiedge (1831 lost)

Der Wanderer (Kerner) (1831, Authenticity not fully proven)

Der Wanderer in der Sägemühle (Kerner) (1832?, Authenticity not fully proven)

An Alexis (For piano or voice? 1832-1833)

Walzer (Lyser) (1834?)

Der Abendstern (1834?)

Am Strande (1840) (Burns, translated by Gerhard)

Ihr Bildnis (Heine) (1840 1st version of Ich stand in dunklen . . .)

Volkslied (Heine) (1840)

Die gute Nacht, die ich dir sage (Rückert) (1841)

Gedichte aus Rückert's Liebesfrühling Op. 12 (1841)

Er ist gekommen in Sturm und Regen (No. 2)

Liebst du um Schönheit (No. 4)

Warum willst du and're fragen (No. 11)

Sie liebten sich beide (Heine) (1842 1st version)

Sechs Lieder Op. 13 (1842-44)

Ich stand in dunklen Träumen (Heine) (1843-44)

Sie liebten sich beide (Heine) (1844 2nd, published version)

Liebeszauber (Geibel) (1842)

Der Mond kommt still gegangen (Geibel) (1842)

Ich hab' in deinem Auge (Rückert) (1843)

Die stille Lotosblume (Geibel) (1842)

Lorelei (Heine) (1843)

Oh weh des Scheidens, das er tat (Rückert) (1843)

Mein Stern (Serre, translated by Wray) (1846)

Beim Abschied (Serre) (1846)

Sechs Lieder aus "Jucunde" von Hermann Rollett Op. 23 (1853)

Was weinst du, Blümlein

An einem lichten Morgen

Geheimes Flüstern hier und dort

Auf einem grünen Hügel

Das ist ein Tag, der klingen mag

O Lust, o Lust

Das Veilchen (Goethe) (1853)

Partsongs:

Schwäne kommen gezogen (1830)

Drei gemischte Chöre (Geibel) (1848)

Abendfeyer in Venedig

Vorwärts

Gondoliera

Orchestra and Chamber:

Scherzo für Orchester (1830-31, lost) Scherzo für Orchester (1830-31, lost)

Piano Concerto in A Minor, Op. 7 (1835-6) [20:57-21:39]

Piano Trio in G Minor, Op. 17 (1846) [24:01-28:44]

Piano Concertino in F Minor (1847) [ca.12:00]

Drei Romanzen for Violin and Piano, Op. 22 (1853) [9:04-11:00]

Piano Concerto in A Minor, Op. 7 (1835-6) [20:57-21:39]

Piano Trio in G Minor, Op. 17 (1846) [24:01-28:44]

Piano Concertino in F Minor (1847) [ca.12:00]

Drei Romanzen for Violin and Piano, Op. 22 (1853) [9:04-11:00]

Piano:

Variationen über ein Tyroler Lied (1830)

Variationen über ein Original-Thema (1830)

Quatre polonaises, Op. 1 (1828-30) [12:58]

Etude (early 1830s)

Phantasie-Variationen über ein Wieck Romanze (1831, lost)

Caprices en forme de valse, Op. 2 (1831-33)

Romance varié in C Major, Op. 3 (1831-33) [9:27]

Rondo in B Minor (1833)

Valses romantiques, Op. 4 (1833-35)

Quatre pièces caractéristiques, Op. 5 (1835-6) [12:33]

Impromptu le sabbat

Caprices a la boleros

Romance

Scene fantastique: le ballet de revenants

Soirées musicales, Op. 6 (1835-6)

Toccatina

Ballade

Nocturne

Polonaise

Mazurka

Mazurka

Variations de concert sur la cavatine du Pirate de Bellini, Op. 8 (1834-37) [15:11]

Souvenier de Vienne, Impromptu in G Major, Op. 9 (1837-8)

Scherzo in D Minor, Op. 10 (1838-9)

Trois romances, Op. 11 (1839) [12:30]

Romance in E-Flat Minor

Romance in G Minor

Romance in A-Flat Major

Sonatina (1841-42, unpub)

Allegro

Scherzo

Adagio

Rondo

Deuxième scherzo in C Minor, Op. 14 (1845)

Quatre pièces fugitives, Op. 15 (1845) [12:12]

Drei Praeludien und Fugen, Op. 16 (1845) [14:39]

Prelude and Fugue in G Minor

Prelude and Fugue in B-Flat Major

Prelude and Fugue in D Minor

Cadenzas for Beethoven: Piano Concerto in G Major, Op. 58 Mvts 1 and 3 (NR: 1846)

Variationen über ein Thema von Robert Schumann, in F-Sharp Minor, Op. 20 (1853) [10:25]

Drei Romanzen, Op. 21 (1853) [10:30]

Romance in A Minor

Romance in F Major

Romance in G Minor

Romanze in A Minor (1853, unpub)

Romanze für Clavier (1855?)

Cadenza for Beethoven: Piano Concerto in C Minor, Op. 37 Mvt 1 (1868)

Geburstagmarsch in E-Flat Major (1879, unpub)

Cadenzas for Mozart: Piano Concerto in D Minor, K466 Mvts 1 and 3 (by 1891)

Vorspiele (Improvisations) (1895, unpub)

Praeludium and Praeludien für Schueler (Improvisations) (1895, unpub)

Picture Sources

The author and publishers wish to express their thanks to the following sources of illustrative material and/or permission to reproduce it. They will make proper acknowledgements in future editions in the event that any omissions have occurred.

Beethoven House, Bonn: pp.54. Archive for Art and History, Berlin: pp13, 34, 62, 64, 68. State Library, Berlin Mendelssohn Collection: pp. 36, 66, 69. City Museum, Braunschweig: pp. 110. National University Library, Dresden: pp.42. Heinrich Heine Institute, Düsseldorf: pp. 53. Lebrecht Music Collection: pp. 72, 74, 76, 82, 92, 99, 127. Robert Schumann House, Zwickau: pp.6, 10, 19, 24, 30, 32, 45, 49, 57, 77, 86, 92, 108, 111, 113, 118, 121, 123, 128. Sotheby's Monaco/Debuisson Collection Paris: pp. 18. The Collection of the Society of Friends of Music, Vienna: pp39. City Library Winterthur: pp. 116. City Museum, Zwickau: pp. 22. Barbara Meier, Dortmund: pp. vi.

Index

40, 67, 70–1, 80, 95–6, 100;
Gewandhaus, 4, 8, 10–12, 23, 28, 53,
55, 57, 70, 97; musical life, 3, 9–10;
Opera, 7; Robert's conducting debut,
58; Robert's works performed, 64, 80;
Schumanns leave, 62
Leipzig, Battle of, 3
Leser, Rosalie, 77
Levi, Hermann, 96, 114
Lind, Jenny, 68, 71
List, Emilie, 23–4, 42–3, 51, 116
List, Friedrich, 24
Liszt, Franz, 28, 52, 56, 96–7, 129;
Clara meets, 19; plays Clara's Op 6,
26, 35; great performer, 32; Clara
plays, 34, 55, 60; influence, 48;
arranges Clara's songs, 75; urges
Clara to avoid salons, 81; on Clara's
playing, 107; *Ave Maria*, 50;
Erlkönig, 47–8; *Hexameron* duo, 55
Litzmann, Berthold, 1
Logier, Johann Bernard, 5
London, 85, 87–9, 94–5, 97, 102, 124;
Clara gives lessons in, 120; Clara's
programme in, 100; pianos in, 109
Lower Rhine Music Festival, 75, 94
Lucerne, 83
Lympany, Moura, 124
Lyon, 93

Magdeburg, 25
manuscripts, 126
Marmorito, Count Vittorio Radicati di,
118
Marschner, Heinrich, 9
Matthay, Tobias, 106
Maxen, 28, 40, 71
Mechetti (publisher), 45
Mendelssohn, Fanny, 69–70
Mendelssohn, Felix, 19, 26, 52–3, 63,
67; Clara plays, 22, 35, 54, 56,
60–1, 69, 76, 88, 90, 96–9; virtually
unknown, 33; helps persuade Robert
visit Russia, 59; Schumanns' relation-
ships with, 61; death, 70; WORKS:
Capriccio in B minor, Op 22, 34,

47, 55, 61; Cello Sonatas, 88; D
minor Trio, 66; *Frühlingslied*, 62;
Piano Concerto in G minor, 60–1,
71, 76; Piano Trio, Op 66, 94; *Rondo
Capriccioso*, Op 14, 97–8; Second
Piano Concerto in D minor, Op 40,
88, 94; *Variations Sérieuses*, 85, 94
Mendelssohn, Paul, 78
Mensing, Professor, 15
Menter, Sophie, 129
Menuhin, Yaltah, 124
Meyerbeer, Giacomo, 19, 42
Mieksch, Johann Aloys, 8
Milchmeyer, Johann Peter, 2
Mitau, 93, 99
Moscheles, Ignaz, 8, 54
Moscow, 61, 93, 97
Mozart, Leopold, 103
Mozart, Wolfgang Amadeus, 8, 45,
96–7, 110–12, 129
Mühlfeld, Richard, 129
Munich, 96

Neue Zeitschrift für Musik, 37, 54; 'Neue
Bahnen' essay, 76
Nikisch, Arthur, 97
Nordeney, 63, 73
Novello (publisher), 129
Nuremberg, 40

Oldenburg, 56
Onslow, Georges, 19, 43
opera, Italian, 60
Orgeni, Aglaja, 115
Ostend, 79, 81

Pacher, Elise, 116
Paer, Ferdinando, 19
Paganini, Niccolò, 9–12
Paris, 17–20, 36, 40, 42–3, 85, 120;
Conservatoire, 91; pianos in, 14;
soirées, 92; vandalised in war, 119
Parish family, 48
Pertzsch, 2
Pest, 81, 90
Pestalozzi, Johann Heinrich, 3

46, 52; works introduced into Clara's repertoire, 22–3, 35; correspondence with Clara, 24, 31, 37, 41, 78, 80, 125; early life, 29; relationship with Wieck, 30, 76; relationship with Ernestine von Fricken, 30–1; relationship with Clara and marriage, 31–2, 37–9, 41, 44, 48–50; mental state, 37, 45–6, 66, 72–3, 77; financial position, 37, 39, 40, 43, 45, 46; legal proceedings against Wieck, 43, 46, 48–9; drinking, 49, 57; marriage diary, 51; health, 51, 57, 61, 63, 69, 72–3, 77; artistic companionship, 54; reconciliation with Wieck, 58; tour of Russia, 59–61; relationship with Mendelssohn, 61; moves to Dresden, 61–3; flees Dresden during uprising, 71; moves to Düsseldorf, 71; professional problems, 72–3; criticisms of Clara, 73; meets Brahms, 75–6; attempted suicide, 77; syphilis, 77; Clara as interpreter, 81, 88, 97, 99, 108–9; death, 2, 82, 113; poor performances of his works, 94; legacy, 125; *Collected Edition*, 125, 127

WORKS: *Papillons*, Op 2, 21; *Impromptus sur une Romance de Clara Wieck*, Op 5, 21, 30; *Davidsbündlertänze*, Op 6, 108; *Allegro*, Op 8, 60; *Carnaval*, Op 9, 35, 48, 81, 89, 90, 92, 94, 99; Piano Sonata in F sharp minor, Op 11, 25, 47, 88; *Fantasiestücke*, Op 12, 60, 69, 80, 97–8; *Études Symphoniques*, Op 13, 32, 80, 81, 93, 99, 104, 105; *Kinderszenen*, Op 15, 47, 88, 109; *Kreisleriana*, Op 16, 90, 94, 98; *Fantasia*, Op 17, 108, 126; *Arabeske*, Op 18, 88; *Novelletten*, Op 21, 48, 54, 102; Sonata in G minor, Op 22, 47; Three Romances, Op 28, 46; Op 32, 97; *Liebesfrühling*, Op 37, 52; First Symphony in G minor, 56; Symphony in B flat major (*Spring Symphony*), Op 38, 54, 60; *Liederkreis*,

Op 39, 59; Piano Quintet, Op 44, 58, 61, 68, 69, 76, 80, 83, 89, 91–2, 94; Andante and Variations for Two Pianos, Op 46, 90, 92; Piano Quartet, Op 47, 92; *Dichterliebe*, Op 48, 100; *Ouvertüre*, Op 52, 55; Piano Concerto (*Phantasie* in A minor), Op 54, 67, 68, 69, 71, 76, 80, 83, 85, 87, 91, 93, 96, 97, 104, 109; Second Symphony in C major, Op 61, 63, 64; Trio in D minor, Op 63, 90; *Album für die Jugend*, Op 68, 105; *Fantasiestücke*, Op 73, 80; Piano Trio, Op 80, 70; *Waldszenen*, Op 82, 88; *Introduction and Allegro Appassionato*, Op 92, 71; Symphony in E flat major (*Rhenish Symphony*), Op 97, 72; Op 99, 74, 97; *Braut von Messina* Overture, Op 100, 97; Violin sonata, Op 105, 92; Fourth Symphony in D minor, Op 120, 55, 97; Violin Sonata in D minor, Op 121, 80; *Schlummerlied*, Op 124, 68, 98; Concerto Allegro for Piano and Orchestra, Op 134, 76, 80; *Das Paradies und die Peri*, 58, 64, 69, 75; *Scenes from Goethe's Faust*, 64; *Genoveva*, 64, 71

Schumann, Therese, 59
Seckendorff, Baron von, 3
Serre, Major, 28, 58, 71
Siebold, Agathe von, 116
Sommerhof, Louis, 128
Spiegel, Oberhofmarschall von, 14
Spohr, Louis, 7, 15
Spontini, Gaspare, 27
Stargardt, 47
Staub, Andreas, 33
Sterndale Bennett, William, 96, 106
Stettin, 47
Stockhausen, Julius, 79–80, 89, 95, 100, 114; Clara's friendship with, 116; response to war, 119
Stockholm, 56
Strauss, Richard, 129
Strobel, Johanna, 5